"I have assigned Rowland Ward's book "*God and Adam: Reformed Theology and the Creation Covenant*" for almost two decades in my Covenant Theology courses at Reformed Theological Seminary. It is the best short survey of the history and development of Reformed opinion on the topic and gets the student up to speed quickly. I am delighted to see it back in print again."

Dr. Ligon Duncan

Chancellor/CEO of Reformed Theological Seminary and the John E. Richards Professor of Systematic and Historical Theology.

"I am delighted to see the republication of this judicious and thoughtful book, which packs an unbelievable amount of information into its relatively few pages! Whether one agrees with all of Rowland Ward's conclusions or not, his balanced account of the contours of Reformed Covenant Theology will be invaluable to anyone thinking through these key issues for biblical and systematic theology."

Dr. Gary Millar

Principal of Queensland Theological College, Brisbane, Australia

"The centrality of the figure of Adam for our understanding of Christ is undeniable and yet Christians are often confused by the myriad of voices competing for their attention on this issue. In this brief work, Rowland Ward clearly and succinctly outlines exactly what is at stake in these discussions and how Reformed theology, summarized and expressed through its confession, has understood the matter of Adam and what theological implications that brings in its wake. A very helpful and easy-to-read work."

Dr. Carl Trueman

Professor of Biblical & Religious Studies at Grove City College, Pennsylvania

"Rowland Ward has written a brief but useful book that explains the covenantal relationship between God and Adam. With few resources on the Covenant of Works, this second revised edition is a welcomed contribution to the on-going discussion on this vital doctrine. Readers would do well to read this work and consult the many cited sources therein and thus sit at the feet of some of the church's greatest theological minds."

Dr. J.V. Fesko

Professor of Systematic and Historical Theology at Reformed Theological Seminary, Jackson, Mississippi

"As Ward shows, Covenant Theology has been a mainstay of reformed theology for over 400 years. It displays the unity of the Bible, shows the depth of the work of Christ and clarifies the relationship of redemption to creation. Yet Covenant Theology is often misunderstood or entirely forgotten in evangelical and reformed circles. *God and Adam* performs a great service by clarifying these key doctrines, and showing how they have been understood in Reformed theology over the centuries—including some of the variations and debates. Ward's comprehensive knowledge of historical Reformed theology, his insightful analysis, and his economic writing makes this a sure guide and an excellent source book. I hope its republication will help to keep alive the flame of classic Covenant Theology."

Dr. John McClean

Vice Principal and Lecturer in Systematic Theology at Christ College, Sydney, Australia

"When Rowland Ward's *God and Adam* first appeared, it made an excellent contribution to Reformed literature. Ward uncovered a wealth of material from the history of Reformed thought and provided thoughtful analysis of many important debates. The revision and expansion of this work in a new edition is a gift to the church. As Ward helps us see, a theologian's view of God's original relationship with Adam is inevitably intertwined with his view of Christ's work and the salvation of his people."

Dr. David VanDrunen

Robert B. Strimple Professor of Systematic Theology and Christian Ethics at Westminster Seminary California

"*God and Adam* is a gem of a resource on Covenant Theology. The summary explanation of covenant is crystal clear—well worth reading even by those new to this great theme in Scripture. Ward gently promulgates classical Reformed theology, not always expressed in violent clash with alternative positions, but safely navigating through difficult waters all the same. Then there is the sheer scale of the historical data that Ward has managed to condense down into manageable size. When one quickly wants to know what the historic Reformed position really is on the covenants, this is the go-to text."

Dr. Jared Hood

Academic Dean and Lecturer in Old Testament at Presbyterian Theological College, Melbourne, Australia

"Beginning with Scripture and working down through history, Rowland Ward's *God and Adam* surveys and summarizes Covenant Theology in three key facets. First, he appropriately frames his examination of Covenant Theology by relating it to wider Christian theology. Scripture, Trinity, creation, anthropology, law, grace, and the doctrine of salvation are all integrated into his insightful presentation. Second, the biblical concept of covenant, its deployment in a pre-fall and post-fall context, and nuanced emphases in the unfolding

Covenant of Grace all receive their theological due. Finally, Ward does not neglect the progressive nature of the church's understanding and misunderstanding of Covenant Theology, but rather educates the reader, as he moves with insightful quotes down though church history from Augustine to N.T. Wright! I know of no better simple and clear introduction to Covenant Theology, giving the careful reader a broad appreciation from beginning of time in Genesis 1 through the beginning of the 21st Century! My students always profit from a perusal of this fine work!"

Dr. W. Duncan Rankin

Adjunct Professor of Systematic Theology at Reformed Theological Seminary, Erskine Theological Seminary, and the Blue Ridge Institute for Theology

"Rowland Ward has written a most helpful work with *God and Adam,* dealing particularly with the contested issue of the existence of the Covenant of Works. Rowland knows the historical background to the debates over this doctrine, which is found in the Westminster Confession, and so proves to be an illuminating guide. Famously, John Murray rejected any notion of a Covenant of Works from Genesis 2:16–17, and Calvin himself was not convinced that Hosea 6:7 referred to any covenant with Adam. On this point at least, neither Calvin nor Murray is convincing, although many have found them so. *God and Adam* is designed to help the reader understand and evaluate this important issue."

Dr. Peter Barnes

Adjunct Lecturer of Church History at Christ College and Pastor of Revesby Presbyterian Church, Sydney, Australia

"It is with great pleasure I commend to you *God and Adam* by Rowland S. Ward. The book helps its readers understand the various issues and nuanced formulations of the Covenant of Works in the literature of Reformed theology primarily in the seventeenth century. It will be of great assistance to those interested in post-Reformation Reformed dogmatics."

Dr. Richard Barcellos

Associate Professor of Exegetical Theology at IRBS Theological Seminary and Pastor of Grace Reformed Baptist Church, Palmdale, California

"God's covenant with Adam and, through him, the whole creation, is a neglected but crucial biblical doctrine. It provides the foundation for a biblical understanding of God's relationship with humankind and with the created world. It is the starting point for a faithful biblical theology, which traces God's purposes from creation to new creation, shaped around the two giants of salvation history, Adam and Christ. And it is a key part of the biblical framework which safeguards a right understanding of God's Covenant of Grace—the gospel of salvation by grace alone, in Christ alone, through faith alone, for the glory of God alone. Rowland Ward's *God and Adam* is the best book-length treatment of this doctrine available. It carefully lays out both its biblical basis, and the history of its recognition in Christian theology. Careful study of this book holds out the promise of a deeper understanding of God and his purposes for human life in the world, and a clearer grasp of the gospel of God's grace in Christ."

Dr. Murray Smith

Lecturer in Biblical Theology and Exegesis at Christ College, Sydney, Australia

"Anyone who wants to understand Covenant Theology need go no further than this book. Rowland Ward has done a superb job explaining the nature of federal theology as it arose in the Reformed tradition with clarity and verve. Take up and read."

Dr. Martin Foord

Lecturer in Systematic Theology at Evangelical Theological College of Asia, Singapore

GOD AND ADAM

REFORMED THEOLOGY
&
THE CREATION COVENANT

ROWLAND S. WARD

GOD AND ADAM
Reformed Theology and the Creation Covenant

For information contact:
Tulip Publishing, PO Box 3150, Lansvale, NSW, Australia 2166
www.tulippublishing.com.au

Book and Cover design by Tulip Publishing

First Edition: 2003
This Revised Edition: 2019

PAPERBACK ISBN: 978-0-6485-3990-2
DIGITAL ISBN: 978-0-6485-3992-6

10 9 8 7 6 5 4 3 2 1

CONTENTS

PART FOUR: COVENANT THEOLOGY, 1701–2000

PREFACE

Presbyterian and Reformed churches have always been interested in the covenant idea, first the covenant of grace in Christ, but also a covenant with Adam before sin, commonly called the covenant of works. But what the covenant of works really meant in the 17th century, when it became standard orthodoxy, is often very poorly understood today. That ignorance has contributed to modifications which are not always for the better.

I think that the structure of Covenant Theology as it developed in the 17th century was essentially on the right lines. More careful exegesis may refine that presentation, but should not lead to it being abandoned. The covenant of works/covenant of grace distinction is not an artificial one unwarranted by Scripture, but a proper distinction which clarifies and safeguards the heart of the gospel in the saving union of the believer with Christ through faith. The impact of confusion or wrong thinking concerning God and Adam, will impact down the line in the understanding of salvation in Christ, the Last Adam.

I could not find a monograph in English on the covenant with Adam which would enable an adequate assessment of the development of covenant thinking prior to 1700.[1]

Hence I have written this small book to fill the gap, and to try and limit divisions among some at the present time, to the extent that misunderstanding or ignorance is causing them.

After an introductory overview, I provide a relatively non-technical presentation of covenant thought loyal to the main lines of the historic Reformed teaching but hopefully taking account of biblical context and historic development in a way that was not usually prominent/possible in the 17th century.

The historical section outlines developments with emphasis on the sources speaking for themselves. My aim is to make the book useful to students and ministers by including translations of materials not easily found, and by adequate citations from original sources. Spelling in older works has been modernised to the extent of removing -eth endings but book titles are original. Not every aspect of the doctrine is considered in detail, but

1 H. Heppe, *Reformed Dogmatics Set Out and Illustrated from the Sources* [1861] trans. G.T.Thomson (Grand Rapids: Baker, 1978) 281–300 is useful but largely omits writers before Cocceius (1648), nor does it show the progress in development. From the viewpoint of systematic theology the section in Herman Bavinck's *Gereformeerde Dogmatiek* from the early 20th century is the best statement of the covenant of works; in English translation as *In the Beginning* (Grand Rapids: Baker, 1999) 197–225. The only monograph I know of is that by N.Diemer, *Het Scheppingsverbond met Adam (het verbond der werken) bij de theologen der 16th, 17th en 18th eeuw in Zwitserland, Duitschland, Nederland en Engeland* [*The Creation Covenant with Adam (the Covenant of Works): theologians of the 16th, 17th and 18th centuries in Switzerland, Germany, The Netherlands and England*] (Kampen: Kok, 1935). This 80 page work is, according to my informant, Rev R.C.Janssen of Nagele, The Netherlands, 'very succinct, almost to the point of being cryptic'. The detailed abstract Dr Janssen provided to me suggests also an overlay of Diemer's own views on the material, and a limited treatment of English writers.

sufficient attention is given on the major areas in order to enable something of the progress in formulating the doctrine to be seen, and for the differences among the orthodox to be recognised. It is thought that quite some light is thrown on the formulation in the Westminster Confession.

Friends and colleagues in several countries have assisted with translations, information or critical review of particular points. They include Dr R. Scott Clark, Rev Gwyn Davies, Dr J. Ligon Duncan, Dr Richard Gaffin, Rev Richard Holst, Rev C. Lee Irons, Dr R.C. Janssen, Dr F. Nigel Lee, Rev Norman Shepherd, Rev Rutger ter Beek, Dr Carl Trueman, Rev Gerald Van Rongen, Rev Cor Vanderhorn, Dr Chad Van Dixhoorn and Dr Noel Weeks. Where appropriate they have been acknowledged in the footnotes. Of course the responsibility for the positions adopted is my own.

The facilities of Monash University in Melbourne, with its microfilm collection of early English books, have been invaluable. Grace Mullen, the ever-helpful Librarian at Westminster Theological Seminary, Philadelphia has located more than one hard to find item. I also record my appreciation to my wife Anna and to the loving congregation of Knox Presbyterian Church of Eastern Australia, Wantirna, Melbourne. This book was commenced about October 2001 and completed on 16 March 2003, the 27th anniversary of my ordination to the gospel ministry.

NOTE FOR SECOND EDITION

The book having fulfilled a need for a basic introduction to Covenant Theology and continuing in demand, it goes forth again in substantially the same form. The most significant differences include greater attention to Particular Baptist views, a rearrangement and expansion of chapter 18 on the Mosaic covenant, some updating in Chapter 25 to take account of recent discussions, and an update of bibliographical references.

Rowland S. Ward

Wantirna, April 2019

"Covenant theology is the Gospel set in the context of God's eternal plan of communion with his people, and its historical outworking in the covenants of works and grace (as well as in the various progressive stages of the covenant of grace)… Covenant theology is the Bible's way of explaining and deepening our understanding of: (1) the atonement [the meaning of the death of Christ]; (2) assurance [the basis of our confidence of communion with God and enjoyment of his promises]; (3) the sacraments [signs and seals of God's covenant promises—what they are and how they work]; and (4) the continuity of redemptive history [the unified plan of God's salvation]…. God's commitments in the eternal covenant of redemption find space-time realisation in the covenant of grace."

Dr J. Ligon Duncan III,

Senior Minister, First Presbyterian Church, Jackson, Miss.

INTRODUCTORY OVERVIEW

The Bible is a covenant book, and its two parts could be better described as the Old Covenant and the New Covenant. The intended contrast is between the covenant with Moses at Sinai and the covenant fulfilled in Jesus Christ 1500 years later, which the old covenant foreshadowed. However, there are other covenant arrangements in the Bible to be considered as well.

Covenant theology understands that God's relationship with humanity always involved a personal, loving, covenant bond, and that God's intention in creation was the rich blessing of the creature he had made in his image. That blessing would come by way of obedience to God's word, although the blessing would be of grace, not wages for work done. The covenant with the First Adam (generally, if not entirely happily, called the covenant of works) was broken, affecting not only Adam but those descending from him in the ordinary way, since humanity forms not merely a physical unity but a spiritual and ethical one also. Adam transmitted a corrupted nature, but his sin was also imputed to his posterity. It was therefore necessary that the obligations of the covenant be met by another, if God's purpose for humanity was to be realised. The suitable substitute was Jesus Christ, the Son of God and the Last Adam. This was in accordance with the agreement or pact between the persons of the Trinity (cf. John 6:37–40;17:1ff), usually called the covenant of redemption. It is the foundation of the covenant of grace made with believers by which, through faith in Christ, they are received back into God's favour—not simply as if they had never sinned but as if they had fully obeyed, as indeed, in Christ they have.

This covenant of grace is God's doing but on man's part it calls for the response of repentance and faith issuing in obedience. These requirements on man's part are not strictly conditions in the sense of things supplied by man to obtain God's blessing as a kind of business contract. Since we are dead in sin we cannot supply them anyway. Rather, they are themselves blessings of the covenant given to the elect on the basis of the work of Christ. The ground of salvation is thus Jesus Christ, God's Son, the obedient Servant, crucified Saviour and risen Lord. Faith in this Christ is the instrumental cause of salvation, the means of receiving it; and good works are fruits of the new relationship, not means of establishing it.

The unfolding of God's gracious covenant is progressive. Covenant theology at its best is keen to pay attention to this historical unfolding of God's purposes. The covenant of grace was given in promise to Adam immediately after he sinned (Gen. 3:15), was continued through Noah (Gen. 6:18; 9:1–17) and formalised with Abraham in the covenant of circumcision (Gen. 17). All believers are beneficiaries of the covenant with Abraham (Gal. 3:7). The special administration adopted in the covenant with Moses (Exod. 19), did not annul the Abrahamic covenant or alter its gracious character (Gal. 3:17ff). The covenant with David to establish his throne forever (2 Sam. 7:12) focused the covenant in a single person. The promise of a new covenant made in Jeremiah's time (Jer. 31 & 33) involves what is foreshadowed in the return from exile being brought to realisation. Christ came in accordance with the everlasting covenant and ratified the new covenant in his blood (Luke 22:20), the climax of God's covenant purpose.

The concept of God's covenants with man came to be a distinctive organising principle in Reformed theology in the 17th century and has had a lasting impact until the present time.[1] However, it would be true to say that real understanding of the structure of this theology is largely absent in conservative evangelical and reformed circles today. That there is a covenant of grace and that Christ suffered in our place are, of course, admitted, but a clear grasp of the biblical context and underpinning of these truths is often lacking. Not infrequently any idea of law as an appropriate part of the relationship between God and man is either vaguely understood or even rejected.

The relationship of Adam and Christ is often poorly perceived. Under pressure from currently popular scientific worldviews, the account of Adam and Eve is regarded as a fictional story without historical basis, or else something a bit difficult to discuss for fear of embarrassment. On the other hand, many conservative Christians have an exaggerated view of the original state of creation. They read the early narratives as if it they were designed to counter 21st century scientific atheists rather than to provide an historical prelude to God's covenant with Moses in the 15th century BC.

---

1 Two accessible classic treatments are 'The Doctrine of the Covenant in Reformed Theology' in G. Vos, *Redemptive History and Biblical Revelation: The Shorter Writings of Geerhardos Vos* (Phillipsburg: Presbyterian & Reformed, 1980), 234–267, and 'Covenant Theology' in John Murray, *Collected Writings of John Murray Vol. 4* (Edinburgh: Banner of Truth, 1982), 216–240. A more recent and well-informed discussion is Joel R. Beeke and Mark Jones, *A Puritan Theology* (Grand Rapids: Reformation Heritage, 2012), 203–318.

The Bible is not an encyclopaedia of the sciences but a distinctly covenant book to teach us the ways of God with humanity. The creation covenant or the covenant of works (or whatever we choose to call it) is a very clear indication that Adam's perfection was not an absolute perfection. He did not yet possess eternal life. He was made as God intended and free from moral evil, but there was glory and honour in prospect too (cf. 1 Cor. 15:44ff).

Unhappily, even those who come from the Presbyterian and Reformed community often have a poor perception of the historic teaching on the covenant of works. One does not object to mere verbal differences,but it is very disturbing to see that quite a number of orthodox writers have the notion that the covenant of works is a merit-based arrangement, the reward being wages earned. But in its formulation of the covenant of works the Reformed tradition has constantly rejected any such idea.

Teaching on the covenant of works historically arose in the 1580s, so that a double covenant scheme, of works and of grace, is characteristic soon after. From the 1630s the covenant of redemption comes to be considered separately from the covenant of grace by a number of writers[2], and this well-recognised difference in presentation was left undecided by the Westminster Assembly in 1646. It continues to this day.

Most of those who wrote on God's covenants in the 17th century gave chief attention to the covenant of grace and to Christ as its Mediator. Treatments of the covenant of works are relatively

2 The elements of the prae-temporal covenant of redemption are found at least as early as Caspar Olevianus (1536–87); cf. L.D. Bierma, *German Calvinism in the Confessional Age* (Grand Rapids: Baker, 1996), 107–112. David Dickson is a Scottish advocate in the 1630s. Its earliest explicit creedal expression is in the Savoy Declaration (1658) 8.1. It is also found in the Baptist Confession (1689) 7.3 & 8.1.

brief. In the English-speaking world Covenant Theology received creedal status in Anglican, Presbyterian, Independent and Baptist Confessions of Faith in the 17th century. Much of the 18th century was rather barren, given the inroads of enlightenment thinking and deism. There was a resurgence in the 19th century, although there has been again a lack of vitality in these circles since, say, 1875.

Outside Britain and Ireland, the creeds of the Reformed churches of Europe did not include specific references to Covenant Theology, as they dated largely from the 16th century. Nevertheless, Covenant Theology was dominant in European Reformed circles to 1700 with significant contributions to the development of covenant thought being made. Its absence from the creeds furthered neglect later, but there was a vigorous revival in the Netherlands from about 1875 under men like Abraham Kuyper and particularly Herman Bavinck (1854–1921). His work remains of great value to this day.

PART ONE
Covenant Theology for Today

"The keynote of the federal theology, as we take it, is UNION WITH CHRIST. Though it took shape as a formal scheme of doctrine or exposition, later than the days of Calvin, it is virtually, through the great predominance and ruling power in the Institutes of the idea of 'union with Christ'—the leading thought in Calvin's theology; far more so than any or all of the 'five' celebrated 'points.' And if this is true: if the heart and soul of this theology is found in the union and communion of Christ and His people; then it is so full of vital power that it will adopt into its service all fresh forms of literary effort and all valid forms of literary culture, and will go on to create more for itself when these are done."

Dr Hugh Martin (1821–85) in The Atonement in its relations to the Covenant, the Priesthood, the Intercession of our Lord (Edinburgh: Knox Press, 1976) 29–30.

1

CREATION AND COVENANT

1. *Kinds of Covenants*

Agreements in human society which enable close relationship and the discharge of mutual obligations may be called covenants. Perhaps we may divide these agreements into two kinds, some more suitably called contracts and the others covenants. Contracts may imply a certain degree of mistrust and may not imply friendship between the parties. Covenants can be thought of as agreements between friends who love each other. Thus, marriage is best described as a covenant rather than a contract. Doing so does not deny the obligation in the pledges made, but suggests a more adequate context for understanding the relationship as one of personal loving commitment.

Covenant is a term that also may be used to describe the relationship between God and his creation. It is used of God's unconditional promise to Noah, and to the birds, livestock and wild animals with him in the ark, in the covenant of the rainbow (Gen. 9:12ff). It is also used of God's commitment to the fixed order of day and night established at creation (Jer. 33:20ff. cf. 31:35). It is more commonly used of God's commitments to people, and calls for appropriate response on their part. The term becomes one of the most significant words in the language of the Old Testament.[1] The climax of a 'new covenant' is reached in Jesus. Indeed, the very terms Old Testament and New Testament are more accurately translated Old Covenant and New Covenant. The Bible is unique in this since other religious traditions do not speak of God making covenant with his creatures.

2. *The Trinity and Humanity*

God does not exist in a vacuum eternally alone. Love, fellowship and faithfulness are at the heart of God, for he eternally exists in a communion of love as Father, Son and Holy Spirit. Made in his image, humans therefore are made to express their lives in love, fellowship and faithfulness to God and their fellow image-bearers. Such is the Christian confession.

Religions drawing from the Bible yet rejecting the Trinity have no consistently logical basis for these qualities of love, fellowship

---

1 The derivation of the Hebrew *berith* (covenant) is still unclear, and the usage in Scripture should not be forced into a single mould such as an agreement involving sacrifice. The arrangement with creation is referred as a covenant in Genesis 6:18 and Jeremiah 33:20 cf 31:35 (discussed on page 15f) yet appears essentially unilateral (although later Noah offers sacrifice). The covenant with Abraham is one-sided in the stipulations yet calls for response by Abraham and in Genesis 15 involves a dramatised curse ritual. The arrangement with David is not described as a covenant in 2 Samuel 7, and it is not associated with a sacrificial ritual, yet it is called a covenant 'cut' with David in Psalm 89:3. The imposition of a single definition of covenant on the material is not warranted although the idea of a binding promise is a constant element.
The ancient covenants and treaties known from extra-biblical sources likewise evidence a variety. They may include a dramatised curse, but only rarely include a sacrifice proper. In the autobiography of the Syrian ruler Idrimi there is mention of a sacrifice in connection with taking an oath (G. Smith, *The Statue of Idri-mi*, London, British Inst of Arch. in Ankara, 1949, 16). However, D.J. Wiseman, 'The Vassal-Treaties of Esarhaddon', *Iraq* 20 (1958), Pt. 1 gives examples for Assyrian treaties and J. Friedrich, *Staatsverträge des Hatti-Reiches* (Leipzig: Hinrichs, 1926), 30 for Hittite ones, without sacrificial ritual. I owe these references to Dr Noel Weeks of the University of Sydney.

and faithfulness since, on their view, they are not reflections of what is true of God. For them God is unitarian, without inner personal distinctions. Unless one advocates the heresy that creation is eternal, God must lack eternal loving relationships, so that love, fellowship and faithfulness cannot be among his essential attributes, and to be like God is to have a life without them.

Hence, vital Christianity has always had an instinctive recognition of the truth of the trinitarian oneness of God, whatever difficulties in formal expression of the doctrine. Thus also she has always recognised the significance of human personality as reflecting the ultimate reality in God himself. The Bible speaks of the three persons of the Trinity in terms of love and fellowship and faithfulness. In God himself there is an ordered relationship, a personal commitment of love, a covenant bond between the Father, the Son and the Holy Spirit. Scripture assures us that this relationship issues also in binding agreements between the Father, the Son and the Spirit. Jesus speaks of an agreement with the Father in accord with which he has come into the world (John 6:37ff cf. Psalm 40:7–8, Heb. 10:5ff). He also speaks of the Holy Spirit who is sent from the Father and the Son as a consequence of the Son's atoning work with a view to rendering it effective in the lives of those whom the Father gave him (John 16:7ff). All that he said and did reflected his undertaking with the Father (John 5:36; 17:4). The Son was ever in a loving relationship with the Father, but he also entered into binding undertakings with him. You have the familial but you also have the legal in what for substance is a covenant relationship, although the actual term is not used.

3. *God's Covenant with Creation*

If we put the question, 'At what point does God begin the covenant relationship with his creatures?' we could answer: When the first world is to be cleansed by a Flood so as to begin anew in Noah, God promises that he will 'confirm' his covenant with Noah (Gen. 6:18). However, the Hebrew term [*heqim*] in this context is that for continuing a relationship not commencing a new one.[2] So there was already a covenant before Noah. When did that covenant begin?

1. That covenant began with creation for, in the aftermath of Noah's Flood, the words of blessing at creation (Gen. 1:28) are repeated (Gen. 9:1–7). By the judgment of the Flood, God has given an illustration of what sin brings, and has begun again with Noah, a kind of second Adam, on a new and cleansed earth like that which had emerged from the waters in creation (Gen. 1:2ff). Hence the original promise in creation is repeated, and is described specifically as a covenant.
2. To the same effect is Jeremiah's reference to God's 'covenant for day and night' (33:20ff). This passage refers back beyond Genesis 9:8 to Genesis 1 and God's blessing of his good creation, as Jeremiah 31:35 makes clear. Thus we see God's covenant commitment at the very beginning of creation.
3. God has a plan for his creation, he is committed to it and he is its Ruler. Covenant in the sense of committed

---

2 W.J. Dumbrell, *Covenant and Creation* (Carlisle: Paternoster, 1984), 25–26 offers a succinct case for this position.

> relationship applies to creation as such, and it comes to a specially focussed expression in the case of humanity.

We must not think of creation in the beginning as a natural order to which is added a supernatural order subsequently so that man can relate to God. A nature/grace dualism is not to be thought of. Rather, all creation is in a dependent relationship to God as its Sovereign, King and Lord. This is the same as saying creation as such is in a covenant relationship since all creation is to live in accordance with the charter given. For humanity, all of life is fundamentally religious because all is lived before the face of God, either obediently in his service or disobediently in the service of an idol.

There is an absolute difference between the Creator and the creation. God is its Originator and Ruler, and it is accountable to him. God administers his rule by way of covenant. As God was not under any obligation to create, and his decision to do so was an absolutely free one, we can speak of a voluntary condescension on God's part. Many older writers, following a view suggested by the Westminster Confession (1646), refer God's voluntary condescension to the act of entering into a covenant with humanity post-creation. This approach could imply humanity was created in God's image but not in covenant, and that God could have withheld his covenant blessing from the creature. I think this would be a somewhat speculative construction that does not mesh well with a careful assessment of Scripture. It risks thinking in terms of a dualism unwarranted by Scripture.

4. *Humanity's Unique Position*

Humans are created in the image and likeness of God, both male and female. In the world of Moses' time the word 'image' can refer to a statue which represented the one imaged. It can also refer to the king as the adopted son of a god fulfilling the role of representing the god in a portion of his kingdom. Genesis shows that the humans are God's in fact vice-regents of a sort[3], called to represent God and to rule over his creation and subdue it to bring out its full potential. The first man is thus correctly recognised as the son of God (Luke 3:38), not his slave. Further, all humans are recognised as bearing God's image, not just the rulers or the nobility. The image or likeness (the terms appear to be interchangeable) is not some spiritual part of man only, but his totality. Note the way Jesus is described as the express image of the invisible God (Heb. 1:3).

The unique relationship with God involved in being God's image, finds expression in the blessing in Genesis 1:28. The ordinance of work and rest provides for humanity's proper relationship to the creation and to the Creator. Labour in God's creation is a blessing not a necessary evil, and the day of rest is a blessing also (Gen. 1:28; 2:3), being made for man (Mark 2:27). Labour has a purpose, and creation has a goal. The seventh day shows that work is not an end in itself, but has its proper place when it is consecrated to God as we subdue the earth in his name. The seventh day represents the goal of history when humanity's work is done and God's rest is entered.[4]

---

3 One should use the term vicegerent (vice-manager/ruler) to avoid the connotation of the ultimate ruler's disability commonly implied in a regency.

4 Karl Barth has at least this point right when he states: 'the goal of creation,

5. *Adam's Limitations*

Creatures other than man are made of the dust of the ground (Gen. 1:24; 3:19) and have the breath of life (7:22) so that they are living beings (1:20; 9:10) as he is. The description in Genesis 2 of the making of the human does highlight the unique position of the man. Still, being from the earth he remains dependent on it. He needs and receives food as surely as fresh air. He needs and receives daylight for labour and night for sleep. He needs and receives a place of sanctuary, where he may worship and obey the LORD so that he may fulfil his task properly in the world beyond the garden with all its rich potential (2:8–15).[5] He needs and receives direction for his life (2:16–17). He needs and receives a woman as a companion and covenant partner (2:18–25). The two become one and the race is multiplied. All these are rich blessings, but these blessings also speak of limitations, of that which is temporary in contrast to the promise of eternal life.

1. The body of dust is capable of dissolution, unlike the incorruptible body of future glory, so in the final kingdom of God the perishable must be supplanted by the imperishable (1 Cor. 15:50).

---

and at the same time the beginning of all that follows, is the event of God's Sabbath freedom, Sabbath rest and Sabbath joy, in which man, too, has been summoned to participate.' Karl Barth, *Church Dogmatics* III/1 (Edinburgh: T & T Clark, 1958), 98.

5 The fitting translation in 2:15 is 'to worship and to obey' rather than 'to work and to keep it'. The standard Hebrew text reads 'to work her and take care of her' and the 'her' cannot be the garden since that is a masculine word. However, some Hebrew manuscripts lack the dot (*mappiq*) in the last letter and that makes the translation infinitive—'to work and to take care' [See U. Cassuto, *A Commentary on the Book of Genesis* (Jerusalem: The Magnes Press, 1961), 122–123]. The usage of the two words for priestly duties—'to worship and to obey'—is recognized by commentators such as Gordon Wenham although its significance is not always followed through adequately.

2. The need for food will not exist in God's ultimate order (1 Cor. 6:13).
3. The regularity of six days of work and one of rest will be superseded when humans enter creation's goal which is God's eternal rest.
4. In the promised glory the possibility of disobedience, sin and death will not be present.
5. Nor will there be marriage or procreation (Matt. 22:30).

Adam is at the beginning of a history with obedience to be given and a reward to be gained. What is natural is first, only later the spiritual (1 Cor. 15:46–47). We must not idealise conditions in the world before sin. The state of innocence in paradise is far surpassed by the state of glory in the new Jerusalem. Put another way, we can say there was an eschatology before there was sin, that is, a glorious destiny was in view of which the tree of life in Genesis 2 was also a token. Creation at the beginning was not like it will be in the end. Then it will be richer and more enduring.

6. *God and the Righteous Adam*

The first Adam was created innocent and holy, in the image of God, with the law of God written on his heart, and therefore God delighted in him and loved him, and the creature likewise delighted in God. Likeness is the basis of fellowship and love. God cannot help loving such a creature just as he cannot but delight in himself. God wants that creature to be a close confidant, a friend, a lover. Once he had determined to create such a creature he could not but desire to share his riches with him. God's purpose with the man was always that there be a committed relationship of love. This kind of relationship is not something incidental or peripheral.

The covenant is the means by which God relates to his creation. The category of love is fundamental but so is the category of law. These categories are not mutually exclusive but complementary. Jesus as God's Son speaks of the mutual love between himself and the Father at the same time as he speaks of obedience to the Father's will. It is not suitable to describe the original relationship of God and Adam as one of love without law nor can it be described properly simply in contract terms. We do not make the separation in a marriage covenant, still less may we in the relationship with God. There are specific contract terms, and if there are blessings in Genesis 1, there is a curse threatened in Genesis 2. Yet the relationship is not and cannot be a mere formal and legal one. Adam had personal communion in righteousness with God from the beginning, and he was to be obedient in the covenant relationship.[6]

---

6 Hosea 6:6–7 declares of Israel that the LORD desired faithful love and the knowledge of God more than sacrifices and offerings, "but they like Adam (or, like man) transgressed the covenant". The rendering "at Adam" is favoured by the parallel in the following line [There they dealt treacherously against me], but "like Adam" or like man/a man is what the Hebrew says. Further, no disobedience at Adam (Josh. 3:16) or Adamah (Josh. 19:36) is known, and the assumption of the passage on this reading is that the disobedience there was notorious. The "There" is thus better taken as a reference to the disobedience in the land God gave them in his covenant (cf. Gen. 12:7). This still leaves a choice between like Adam and like man/a man but either way a parallel between Adam/man and Israel is being drawn, thus a breaking of a covenant with God in both cases, rather than covenants with other men in the case of Adam/man and a covenant with God in the case of Israel. The point will then be: Adam broke the covenant God made with him and was driven from Eden; Israel has broken the covenant God made with her and will be driven out of the land God gave her, cf.

The covenant relationship at creation is expressed in a highly focused form in a specific arrangement with Adam described in Genesis 2:16–17. In this arrangement the common idea is present of a covenant as an agreement involving mutual faithfulness to the stated obligations, and for the lesser party (man), to receive a blessing of great richness from the greater party (God). It is true that the promise is not explicit in these verses, but the threat of death for disobedience implies the promise of life for obedience, and several features already noted in the context say the same. These include the blessing of humanity at creation (Gen. 1:28), the blessing of the seventh day as representing creation's goal, and the tree of life in the garden.

One could add to them the remarkable use of the term LORD God (20 times) in Genesis 2–3. This is used only 16 times elsewhere in the Old Testament. The emphasis of the name is that the Creator (God) is also covenant partner of his people (LORD).[7]

One can look at the relationship from different angles. As the original relationship it may be called the covenant of creation. As it was to be fulfilled by man in the strength with which he is endowed it may be called the covenant of nature. Being made with Adam before sin it may be called the covenant of innocence. As made between parties who were friends it may be called the covenant of friendship. The blessing in view may lead us to call it a covenant of life, while the requirement of obedience to God suggests the

---

Hos. 1:9. Despite Calvin's assessment of like Adam as "vapid", this does appear the proper choice given that Scripture attests a covenant relationship with Adam. Covenant theologians did not rest their case on Hosea 6:7. See further footnote on page 57.

7 See the discussion in Gordon J. Wenham, *Word Biblical Commentary 1: Genesis 1–15* (Waco: Word Books, 1987), 56–57. Note that neither the serpent nor the woman use this name (LORD God) in Genesis 3:1–5, when God's faithfulness is being questioned.

term legal covenant, covenant of obedience or covenant of works. Consideration of the tender love and generosity God showed may suggest the term covenant of favour. A more neutral term could be Adamic covenant.

I remain mindful of the problems of terminology, but the terminology is not the issue. The distinctive significance of the Adamic covenant is the issue, and it must be seen as one requiring obedience to the covenant terms as the principle required in order to the blessing. In Protestant theology covenant of works has been the common expression and is contrasted with the covenant of grace instituted after the entry of sin. The covenant of grace is not a separate covenant so much as that development necessitated by the fact that God, confronted by sin, does not abandon his covenanted commitment to his creation but relates to it redemptively.

7. *God's Direction to Adam*

Although the creature was very good, that is, just as God intended, it was possible for Adam to turn aside from his holy state. Life and death were set before him, blessings and curses, as we have seen. The other class of moral beings of which we have some knowledge, the angels, were in the same position too. However, they were not created as a race but as individuals. In their testing some fell and some stood firm (2 Pet. 2:4). This suggests that a creature with a moral nature must freely say its 'Amen' to God if it is to be confirmed in its relationship to him. Put another way, we may reverently say that, so far as we are aware, God could not create a moral creature free from the possibility of disobedience. God is motivated by love: 'God is love' (1 John 4:6). The creature made in God's image in turn responds to God not through force but in love and freely. But if the creature is free the possibility of disobedience exists.

How can humans be brought to a position where the possibility of disobedience no longer exists? Those who are required to obey God perfectly anyway, can never bring God under obligation. In this light, when the creature has done everything, he has, as it were, earned his keep but he has not put God in his debt. A long course of obedience would still leave the creature with the possibility of disobedience, so ultimate security and bliss could never be certain.

Now if God as the supreme Lover desires the best for the one he loves, an intimate and lasting friendship crowned with all the blessings he can bestow, he could grant a reward of eternal fellowship as a consequence of obedience to the covenant terms. For although we grant that man can never stand before God in his own merit as if he has acquired rights, he can stand before God as an obedient covenant son and claim the reward God promised when he bound himself to the man in covenant.

Suppose a father says to his son that although he is obliged to be obedient to him he will give him a special benefit if he is careful to be good during the holidays, has he done something unjust? He has not promised something as of right as a reward, but he has promised a reward in terms of a covenant. Has he acted in an arbitrary way? No, for a father loves his son and wants the fullest blessing for him. Just so, the Heavenly Father wants his son, made in his image, to have the fullest blessing. If the desire of the Father to bless his son is complemented by the son's desire to please his father, then the covenant obedience is crowned by the promised blessing. The issue in this scenario is not merit as such but the provision of a reward for obedience in terms of the covenant commitment. The obedience gives the right to the reward.

The above is the viewpoint of the mainstream of covenant theologians from the earliest mature expression of the two-covenant scheme in 1597 by the Scot, Robert Rollock, to the well-nuanced position of Dutch theologian Herman Bavinck around 1897. And of course this form of Covenant Theology is a natural development of what is implicit or explicit in the position of the 16th century Protestant Reformers as well, not to speak of the early Church Fathers.

2

THE BIBLICAL UNFOLDING OF THE COVENANT

Adam was made a king or ruler of the earth under God, and placed in a central sanctuary garden reminiscent of later priestly sanctuaries in Israel. Since the moment of Adam's disobedience restoration to God's fellowship by our obedience is impossible; we are shut up to reliance on another, Jesus Christ. He is in fact called the Last Adam (1 Cor. 15:45) as well as 'the first born from the dead and the Ruler of the kings of the earth' (Rev. 1:5). This is as much as to say that there have been several Adams after Adam who did not fulfil the promise of the seed of the woman who would crush the serpent's head (Gen. 3:15). Eventually came one who did meet every requirement and who is not succeeded by any other. This one, Jesus Christ, brings the new humanity into its true position as 'a kingdom of priests to serve his God and Father' (Rev. 1:6).

Given Adam's breaking of the covenant of works, the covenant of redemption operates to provide a covenant of grace for us. In accordance with the terms of the covenant of redemption with the Father, Christ was fully obedient and thereby fulfilled Adam's covenant of works and secured the Holy Spirit for his people. Paul speaks of believers having been under the curse of a broken law but, he says, 'Christ redeemed us by becoming a curse for us' (Gal. 3:13). 'God sent his Son, who was born of a woman, born under law, to redeem those who were under law, that we might receive the full rights of sons' and that the Holy Spirit might be given to us (Gal. 4:5–6).

In this chapter a basic outline of the theme of God's covenant purposes is given.

1. Adam - the Covenant of Creation

In Genesis 1–7 God brings forth the earth from water, reducing chaos to order. He appoints Adam ruler of the earth. The goal of creation is to share God's rest. God places man in his presence in a sanctuary garden, under his covenant, showing him how his dominion must be exercised to be effective. Adam disobeys. The nakedness of this sin God covers by coats of skins, and he is expelled to the east. One is promised who will destroy the works of the devil. Meantime, we see the fruit of Adam's sin in his descendants, and the ultimate judgment of the flood, a reversal of creation, with a remnant saved in the ark.

In the promise to Adam (Gen. 3:15) God continues his commitment to creation: the Serpent will be crushed by the woman's seed. But Cain turns out not to be that seed: he is on the side of the Serpent. Productive achievements in terms of livestock management, music and metal-working are noted (Gen. 4:19ff), but are associated with spiritual decline—Lamech's polygamy and arrogant sword-song. Even Seth does not prove to be the foundation of a better future: his line also descends into wickedness.

The judgment of the Flood means that creation returns to something like the watery formless mass at its beginning. Noah's Flood is a picture of the ultimate judgment at the end of the world that Enoch spoke about (cf. Jude 14). The New Testament uses it to point to the end of this order and the introduction of a new heaven and a new earth, the home of righteousness (2 Pet. 3:6–7,10–13).

2. *Noah – the Covenant of the Rainbow*

Genesis 8–11 is a redemptive re-enactment. The world is recreated out of the waters of the flood, reducing chaos to order. God appoints Noah (Gen. 6:18; 7:1) head of this new creation and continues his creation covenant with him (Gen. 8:15–20). Noah's name is from the Hebrew root *nuah*, to rest (cf. Gen. 5:29). Noah plants a vineyard where he sins in drinking to excess. The nakedness of this sin two of his sons cover with a garment. The fruit of Noah's sin is seen in his descendants, particularly the wicked citizens of Babel who aim to make a name for themselves through cultural achievements. However, ultimate judgment is postponed for it is God's determination to fulfil his covenant with creation.

It is 'righteous' Noah (6:6; 7:1) who heads up a new creation as a kind of new Adam, but it was because he found grace in God's sight (6:5), not that he was inherently righteous. God pledges to continue his covenant with him (6:18). God preserves him and his family in the ark, 'remembers' his covenant with him (8:1) and so, by a strong wind reminiscent of the moving of the Spirit on the face of the waters in 1:3, dries up the waters so that dry land appears. When Noah steps out on a new and cleansed earth, the covenant of the rainbow is confirmed in terms which echo unmistakeably the blessing of creation in Genesis 1:28, and which speak just as clearly of God's unilateral determination to continue his purposes to bring creation to its goal. The rainbow is to 'remind' God of his purpose, a powerful way of saying that God will act to ensure his purpose is fulfilled.

There will be no further Noah-like Flood since it cannot eradicate the sin in the human heart (8:21). Noah offers a burnt offering in sacrifice. However, between the reiterated blessing of human fruitfulness in 9:1 and 9:7 are several new points. They amount to provisions to advance respect for human life by protecting it (vv2, 4–6) and sustaining it (v3). They are laws to be obeyed that will not be irrelevant for the later system of sacrifices in Israel.

But Noah is himself part of the problem (9:20–21). He is not able to bear the weight of the world's redemption. Noah cannot bring that rest of which his name speaks and which is creation's goal. As Adam's sin had resulted in division among his descendants, so does Noah's sin. As Adam and Eve's eyes were opened unaided, so Noah seems to know what had happened without being told. Whereas God judged Adam and Eve, Noah exercises the authority given in 9:6 and utters predictions in terms of a curse on part of his family and blessings for others. The Serpent was cursed and so was Cain. Now Canaan is cursed too. It is as if the Canaanite peoples represent the Serpent's seed, and thus their historic overthrow by Israel is justified. It is a picture of the ultimate judgment of all workers of evil.

The other two sons receive blessings but Shem is given the pre-eminence without anything stated as the basis of the preference.

This points to the sheer unmerited favour of God. He chooses Shem, apparently the youngest son (10:21), rather than Japheth. Shem means name. But if Shem's line is the favoured one, progress still seems to be downward. The Tower of Babel episode is a re-run of times before the Flood: man without God is a clever devil. Men suppose to make a name for themselves. In effect they think that they can reach up to God's throne, access the power and authority of heaven, and use it for their own glory. The desire for unity and a city is not of itself wrong. God has a plan for unity and for a city too, but it does not come on the foundation of human sin but through its overthrow, and the establishing of righteousness. In mercy and in judgment, God limits the cruel power of man and scatters the builders. Yet Shem's descendants end up in the Babel-like civilisation of Ur as idolaters (Josh. 24:2). Only the fact of God's commitment to his creation means that all is not lost. There will be another new Adam.

3. *Abraham – the Covenant of Circumcision*

Genesis 11:27–50:26 records a more developed redemptive re-enactment in the events in the family line of Abraham, Isaac and Jacob. God's choice of Abram occurs in the context of the disunity of humanity and the impression God's creation covenant will fail. That would be a wrong impression for the choice of Abram is with a view to the fulfilment of the creation covenant. Abram and the descendants God gives him are to be a means of bringing the covenant blessings to the whole world.

Abram is like a dead man, his name (meaning proud father) a mockery, for he has no children and his wife is barren (Gen. 11:30). But God calls into being things that are not (cf. Rom. 4:17), and he commands Abram to leave his father's house and go to a land he will show him. In contrast to the Babel builders, God will act to make Abram a great nation, to bless him, to make his name great, decide the fate of men on how they relate to him, and to bless the whole world through him (Gen. 12:1–3). It will be 25 years before Abram has the child of the promise (Gen. 12:4;17:1,21), and his faith was tested. Yet he believed the LORD and it was reckoned to him as righteousness (Gen. 15:6). The thought is not that faith is meritorious, but that the one in whom Abram trusted provides for him the righteousness he needs as the basis of fellowship, a righteousness he receives as God's gift through faith.

A year before Isaac's birth God formalises his promise in the covenant of circumcision. Abram's name is changed to Abraham, father of a multitude, because God's blessing will result in him being the father of nations and of kings (Gen. 17:1ff). Whereas in 1:28 God had said to Adam and Eve, 'Be fruitful and multiply', and similarly to Noah and his sons in 9:1, the emphasis now is different. God says to Abraham, 'I will make you very fruitful' (17:6). The heart of the covenant is God's total commitment: 'I will be your God and the God of your children after you'. The New Testament does not provide any greater promise, but rather discloses the implications of God's commitment. Abraham is also assured of possession of the land of Canaan as a free gift.

We find therefore no total lapse in Abraham. He is kept by the power of God. God does not favour him because he is worthy but because God is gracious and provides righteousness for him. He is promised greatness by God, not rewarded for already existing greatness. God's total commitment to Abraham is shown ultimately in the gift of God's son as the true and Last Adam.

Adam was given the whole earth to subdue whereas Abraham is promised the land of Canaan as God's gift (15:7; 17:8). Nevertheless, all nations will be blessed through Abraham (12:3 cf. Gal. 3:8). When the writer to the Hebrews speaks of Abraham looking beyond Canaan to a new creation (Heb. 11:9–10,16), he writes perceptively, for Canaan has replaced the whole earth only temporarily and typically. Abraham is the inheritor of the creation covenant as a new Adam. As Paul puts it, Abraham inherits the world (Rom. 4:13). The inclusiveness of the church composed of both Jews and Gentiles, which is so insisted upon in the New Testament, reflects the reality of all believers, all true children of Abraham, as God's new human family united in Jesus Christ, the Last Adam.

There is a dramatised curse ritual in connection with the covenant with Abraham when God confirms his promise of the land (15:8–20). God will be dismembered if he does not keep his promise! There is also obligation on Abraham. He is to walk before God Almighty and be perfect (17:1), and the rite of circumcision is the sign of God's covenant, the expression of his obedience, and the call to continue walking before the LORD.

The covenant formalised with Abraham continues through Isaac (26:3f) and on to Jacob (35:11). The continuation of the covenant is of God's grace, for Isaac's wife is also barren (25:21) and so is Jacob's wife, Rachel (29:31), ultimately the mother of Joseph; it is also contrary to nature since the birthright is carried on by the younger: Jacob not Esau, Joseph not Reuben, Ephraim not Manasseh.

In Joseph's life in particular, there is the beginning of a provisional fulfilment of the promise to Abraham: God is with Joseph in everything (Gen. 39:20–23). Although he has many trials and his name seems to be cut off, yet his name is made great, and he becomes a blessing to the nations of 'all the earth' (Gen. 41:56 – 57). Reckoned as the first born of his many brothers (49:22ff), he delivers and protects the children of Abraham. But as yet they are a nation only in embryo. Nevertheless, they prosper numerically and materially during their time in Egypt (47:27; Exod. 1:7) until a Pharaoh came to the throne who cared nothing for Joseph's work. He makes the Hebrews slaves, and orders their male babies to be killed at birth. It looks like the end. But then there is another new beginning. God's covenant word brings hope.

4. Moses and the Covenant at Sinai

The Book of Exodus speaks of God's acts in terms of a new creation. Moses, like Noah, was saved in an ark from drowning so as to bring salvation to others. [The rare Hebrew word *teba* is used only of Noah's boat and Moses' basket, both presumably made of reeds covered with pitch.] Israel is God's firstborn son (Exod. 4:22) like Adam (cf. Luke 3:38), created by God (Isa. 43:1) and saved from the waters of judgment that engulfed the Egyptians at the Red Sea after the plagues had reduced their ordered world to a waste (cf. Gen. 1:2). Israel is God's new Adam, God's new humanity.

We read that God 'remembered' his covenant with Abraham (Exod. 6:5), and therefore delivered the Israelites from their oppressors in Egypt: he cursed the Egyptians but blessed his people. It is important to note that this act of grace was not apart from the provision of a sacrifice in the Passover lamb. In the houses of the Egyptians the first-born died; in the houses of the Israelites a lamb dies. Israel as a whole, God's firstborn son, exits the bondage of Egypt into freedom under God.

The initial goal of their journey is Horeb or Mt Sinai (Exod. 3:1,12).[1] When they arrive Moses receives God's law, which the people affirm they accept and will obey. Then the people are sprinkled with the blood of the covenant (Exod. 24:1–9). Those who are already covenant people are thus committed to God's law, but their inevitable failure in obedience will not overthrow the covenant because of the provision of the sprinkled blood.

God brought them to the land he had promised to Abraham generations before, giving them victories over the Canaanites so that they could settle in the land and experience rest (Deut. 12:10; Josh. 21:43–45). The curse of Canaan is being worked out, and God's determination to put enmity between the seed of the woman and the seed of the serpent is demonstrated (Gen. 3:15), as also his determination to make for Abraham a great name and a great nation. It is all of grace.

Prior to Exodus 19:3, Scripture is a kind of prologue to the covenant then made at Sinai[2] by which Israel, already belonging

---

1 In Exodus 3:18 the request for a three day journey appears part of the bargaining process typical in an Eastern context, cf. John L. Mackay, *Exodus* (Fearn: Mentor, 2001), 81,104. The journey to Mt Sinai actually took about three months (Exod. 19:1).

2 A helpful analysis is in David A. Dorsey, *The Literary Structure of the Old*

to God, is committed to become a kingdom of priests, a fully sanctified nation (Exod. 19:4–6). A detailed system of ritual or ceremonial law was also imposed, including a system of symbolic sacrifices to deal with sin. Strikingly, there appear no sacrifices for wilful sin, sin 'with a high hand', such as David's adultery. For these there was nothing but the covenant mercy of God (Psalm 51:1), which in fact underpinned the entire life of the nation.

A generation later the covenant is renewed before entry into the Promised Land. The book of Deuteronomy reviews the past (chs. 1–4), reiterates the Ten Words we commonly call the ten commandments (5), expounds and applies them in order (6–26), provides for reaffirmation of the covenant (27–30), and for its continuation (31–34).[3] The commandments given to Israel by God cover all aspects of life, not just narrowly religious matters, and they are to be kept in the context of response to God's gracious deliverance of his people. Obedience is a necessary fruit of the covenant relationship with God, not a means of establishing it. For Israel it is all of grace because God is faithful to his covenant.

As the new Adam, Israel—which can mean Prince with God—is brought into the new Eden, entering it from the east which was guarded by a mysterious angel with a sword (Josh. 5:13). This reminds us of the cherubim on the east of Eden who guarded the way to Paradise (Gen. 3:24). The new Eden is a land flowing with milk and honey where the new Adam is to be fruitful and multiply (Gen. 1:28; Deut. 6:3; 8:6ff), living under God's covenant.

Testament (Grand Rapids: Baker, 1999), 70.

3 I have followed the outline in Allan M. Harman, *Deuteronomy: The Commands of a Covenant God* (Fearn: Christian Focus, 2001).

At this point a difficulty is sometimes felt. The new Adam's continuance in the land of Canaan depends on his obedience to that covenant as did the first Adam's continuance in Eden. There are blessings for obedience, and curses for disobedience (Deut. 28); 'life and prosperity, death and destruction' is set before Israel (Deut. 30:15). If Israel disobeys she will be expelled to the east once more, to Babylon, or returned to captivity in Egypt. 'Is not Israel actually under a covenant of works?' one may ask.

However, as we have seen, it is fundamental that Israel is not received into God's favour because of obedience but because of God's gracious covenant with Abraham. The law of Moses has not overthrown the covenant promise of God to Abraham (Gal. 3:17). Covenant and law are differently related. Noah, saved from the Flood by God's grace, received God's law (Gen. 9:1ff). Abraham, justified through faith, was to walk before God and be perfect (Gen. 17:1). Similarly, redeemed Israel receives God's law, although in much more elaborated form than previously, so that she might be a holy nation (Exod. 19:6). The exhortation to New Testament believers by the One greater than Moses is the same: 'Be perfect as your Heavenly Father is perfect' (Matt. 5:47). The giving of law to the redeemed of God reflects the fact that obedience to the covenant Lord is always the appropriate response of the redeemed. The demand of law, and the pressing toward the mark, does not imply that in this life perfect obedience will be achieved, or that we are justified on the basis of works.

Israel is the subject of grace just because it is impossible for righteousness to be obtained by Israel's obedience. The addition of the Mosaic law instructs the people in God's character, but multiplies the opportunities for sin, convicts and restricts with a view to preparing the people for the One who would crush the Serpent's head (Gal. 3). In this sense the Mosaic covenant is both gracious and burdensome (cf. Acts 15:10). At the same time the law holds out the promise of life for perfect obedience. 'If you would enter into life keep the commandments' is a faithful saying (Matt. 19:17), even if it is only a theoretical possibility for sinners. Paul rightly stresses: 'If righteousness could be gained through the law, Christ died for nothing' (Gal. 2:21)

There was a peculiarity for Israel since her existence as a nation provided a pattern and a portrayal on the physical level of the reality of the Kingdom of God to be realised in Jesus Christ. Canaan being a picture of the heavenly country (Heb. 11:16), it cannot continue to be possessed by a covenant-breaking people. Hence, on the temporal level, the fortunes of Israel are tied to her spiritual faithfulness (but note Psalm 44:9ff). This feature also emphasises the necessity of perfect obedience in order to inherit God's rest, and so encourages the expectation of the promised seed of Abraham, the true Passover Lamb.

Adam had been made as ruler of the earth, and God's purpose is that the goal of creation will be fulfilled despite the entry of sin. So humanity must again rule effectively. Israel was to be a kingdom of priests (Exod. 19:4–6), ruling for God in fellowship with him. However, in the absence of a king each person did what seemed right in his own eyes (Jdg. 17:6; 21:25). They fell into religious syncretism (Jdg. 17) and Sodom-like depravity (Jdg. 19:16ff cf. Gen. 19:1ff), and their enemies plundered them. Only through God's gift of kingship could God's purpose be realised.

5. *David and the Kingdom Covenant*

The Lord in mercy (1 Sam. 9:16) yields to the people's wrongly motivated desire for a king by giving them one (Saul) who outwardly appeared ideal—a head taller than anyone else (1 Sam. 10:23)—but who proved a failure in the end. David, God's replacement for Saul, was not the likely choice. Even Samuel thought David's older brother was the obvious candidate (1 Sam. 6:6–7). But the LORD said: 'Do not consider his appearance or his height, for I have rejected him. The LORD does not look at the things man looks at. Man looks at the outward appearance, but the LORD looks on the heart.' God's choice was David, a man who feared the Lord and hoped in his mercy. In the contest with Goliath (1 Sam. 17) the lesson is enforced. Man's choice leads to fear and failure. God's choice, though outwardly of one of little account, will bring God's people deliverance and a mighty victory over their enemies. God continued his covenant to David.

The arrangement with David as recorded in 2 Samuel 7:1ff is not in fact described as a covenant. However, like the arrangement in Eden, it has all the features of a covenant, and is described as such elsewhere in Scripture (e.g. Psalm 89:3). It is also noteworthy that the unusual form of God's name (LORD God) found in Genesis 2 is also found in 2 Samuel 7 (refer to page 13).

God's promise to David includes terms which bring the previous promises to mind: the promise of a great name (7:9), a place for Israel to call home (7:10), freedom from oppression and rest from all enemies (7:11–11), a future seed (7:12) who will be God's son (7:14), and the linking of the choice of Israel as God's own with the establishing of David's kingdom for ever (7:24,16). Clearly, God's blessing to Abraham is to be fulfilled through David's line. As the formless and empty earth had been formed and filled by the Great King, with his son Adam placed in it as image and ruler, so God will make a house for David that his son may rule in peace and righteousness. In turn, David's son will build God's House where God may dwell in the midst of his people. God will relate to him as a father to his son. Individuals may be chastised but David's dynasty and kingdom will be eternal.

David's reaction is striking. The difficult phrase in 7:19 is commonly translated 'Is this your usual way of dealing with man, O LORD God?' The verse is David's response to God's revelation, and reads literally, 'This is the law (or charter) [*torah*] of humanity, O LORD God'. This fits the context perfectly. David recognises that God's promise through him secures the future of humanity.[4] One will arise from David's line to fulfil the promise made to Abraham, overthrow the Serpent, and bring about the goal of creation, God with his people forever. Israel is to be concentrated in one representative person.

Several passages in the Psalms point to God's special son as the true occupant of David's throne (e.g. Psalm 110:1; 45:7) and God's "firstborn" (Psalm 89:27). Indeed, David's throne was really God's throne (1 Chron. 29:22). A preliminary fulfilment comes in David's son Solomon. He has a reign of outward splendour and peace (c. 970–931 BC), and is acknowledged among the nations for his wisdom and the glory of his kingdom. Yet he is not the perfect king; the kingdom is split into two after his death, and

4 Walter Kaiser's discussion in J.H.Skilton (ed.), *The Law and the Prophets* (Nutley: Presbyterian & Reformed, 1974), 298–318 is recommended. In the parallel in 1 Chronicles 17:17, the text is somewhat obscure. It reads in literal form, 'And you are regarding me as a law of humanity the uplifting'.

his successors experience the promised chastisement. The true fulfilment awaits the coming of David's greater son, who is also David's Lord (Psalm 110:1 cf. Matt. 22:41–45).

The decline of the nation continued. Two hundred years after David, Isaiah anticipates the defeat of the people and their exile to a foreign land. Exile to Assyria or to Babylon will be like slavery in Egypt. In 722 BC the ten northern tribes, who had rebelled against the Davidic dynasty after Solomon's death, were defeated by the Assyrians. Many of the people were forcibly resettled elsewhere in the Assyrian Empire. The two remaining tribes (Judah and little Benjamin) did not follow the LORD rightly either. Things were going from bad to worse. Where is the promised King, the promised Son of God? Where is the faithful Servant, the Redeemer from sin?

Beginning about 605 BC the people of Judah came under the control of the Babylonian Empire. Some, like Daniel, were deported to Babylon. Jerusalem itself was destroyed in 586 BC, and many more Jews taken into captivity. The principle was simply that Israel had not kept God's covenant law, and the land had not enjoyed its sabbath rest for 490 years. It would now have 70 years of enforced rest (2 Chron. 36:21) in line with the principle set out with startling clarity in Leviticus 26 (note verses 33–35). Thus Israel was banished from the land for her sins, just as Adam and Eve had been banished from the Garden. All again seemed dark and hopeless. No temple, no king, no land.

But God! Covenant restoration after covenant disobedience is also set out in Leviticus 26. 'I will remember my covenant with Abraham... I will remember the covenant I made with their ancestors whom I brought out of Egypt.' Thus Isaiah says that not only will there be a new captivity, there will also be a new exodus

(Isa. 43:16–29; 48:20–21; 51:9–11). A remnant will return to form the nucleus of a new Israel through the Lord's anointed one/messiah. This messiah is specifically identified by name as Cyrus (Isa. 45:1). The work of this Persian king (c. 585–529 BC) provides an illustration of the work of God's true anointed one/messiah, the son of David, the crusher of the Serpent.

Around 732 BC Isaiah speaks to the house of David of a child born of a virgin who will be called Immanuel, God with us, and who will rule on David's throne for ever (Isa. 7:13–14; 9:6–7). He also speaks of a righteous servant, equipped by God's Spirit, who brings justice to the nations (42:1–6). This servant is identified with God yet distinguished from him (50:1–3,14–17). The servant is not Cyrus, who is plainly stated to be an unbeliever (45:4). The servant in view will suffer for the sins of the unfaithful people to remove their guilt. Here, surely, is the seed of the woman who will overthrow the Serpent.

From about 626 BC the prophet Jeremiah spoke God's word to the people although it was not well received. Who would save the remnant of God's covenant people? Exile was certain. God's promise of commitment to his covenant alone gave hope. There would be a new covenant.

6. *Messiah and the New Covenant Prefigured*

Jeremiah, like Isaiah, had recognised the failure of the theocracy; her day of earthly glory was past. He predicts 70 years of captivity in Babylon (Jer. 25). The fundamental relationship of God to Israel will be realised somewhat differently in the future, and it depends upon God's work. God would raise up a wise and righteous king from David's line who would bring peace to Judah and Israel, and who would be called 'The LORD our Righteousness' (Jer. 23:5–6). In effect Jeremiah expands Isaiah's prophecy of the child born of a virgin with 'Mighty God' as one of his names. Jeremiah also speaks of a new covenant that God would make with his people that would ensure God's law was written on their hearts. He spoke about return from captivity (Jer. 30:1ff), and the rebuilding of a Jerusalem that would be truly holy (Jer. 31:38ff), of a reconstituted house of Judah and house of Israel under a new covenant (31:31).

Ezekiel, taken to Babylon in the second deportation of 597 BC, speaks of a judgment that cannot be escaped, and of the overthrow of the temple (which occurred at the hands of Nebuchadnezzar in 586 BC). But he also is sure that God will restore his people. If Israel seems to be like a valley of dry bones, God by his Spirit can revive her (Ezek. 37). Indeed, he will unite Israel and Judah into one nation under a Davidic king according to his covenant of peace (Ezek. 37:15–28). He will put his Spirit in his people so that they keep his law (Ezek. 36:27–28), and will return the land to Eden-like conditions (Ezek. 36:35). There will be a wonderful new temple, and the glory of God will enter it through the gate facing east (Ezek. 43:1–5).

About 540 BC Daniel read Jeremiah's writings (Dan. 9:2) in Babylon, and prayed accordingly. 2 Chronicles 36:21 explains that the number of years of exile corresponded to the number of years the land had not enjoyed the sabbath it was due each seven years (cf. Lev. 25).[5] Daniel's prayer (9:3–19) is the prayer of one who knows

5 How the 490 years without observance of the sabbath for the land is calculated is unclear. If we go back in an unbroken line from 605 BC, we reach 1095 BC, which is before King David's reign (c. 1010–970 BC.).

the nation has lost privileges of the covenant—the temple and sacrificial system, the city of Jerusalem and life in a land flowing with milk and honey—because of covenant disobedience. 'But if they will confess their sins and the sins of their fathers...I will remember my covenant....I will remember the land' (Lev. 26:40ff. cf. Deut. 30:1ff.).

The human deliverer of the covenant people was the ruler of the Medes and Persians, a man named Cyrus,[6] just as predicted by God through Isaiah (Isa. 45:1). He and his men overthrew the Babylonian Empire in October 539 BC, and allowed the resettled peoples to return to their own lands. It was a new beginning, life from death. Cyrus was not the promised seed of the woman but he provided a picture of the promised seed in the way in which he brought God's people's bondage to an end and allowed them to return to their own land. By 516 BC the temple had been rebuilt under Haggai (Ezra 6), and Jerusalem's wall was also rebuilt in the time of Nehemiah, probably 445 BC.

Psalm 126 sings:

> 1 When the LORD brought back the captives to Zion,
> we were like men who dreamed.
> 2 Our mouths were filled with laughter,
> our tongues with songs of joy.
> Then it was said among the nations,
> 'The LORD has done great things for them.'

---

6 The relationship of Cyrus and Darius, the ruler named in Daniel 5:30, is debated. The ancient non-biblical records show that there is something unusual about the first year or two of Cyrus' rule. It has been suggested, by the noted Assyriologist D.J.Wiseman, that Darius could be an alternative name for Cyrus, or perhaps Darius is the name of a sub-ruler under Cyrus as suggested by W.H.Shea.

3 The LORD has done great things for us,
and we are filled with joy.

The return from exile is certainly fulfilment of Jeremiah's prediction (Jer. 30:3), as is the rebuilding of Jerusalem (Jer. 31:38–40). But Jerusalem does not turn out to be fully holy in terms of the prediction, nor, despite religious renewal under Nehemiah, were all the people sincere believers—although their fondness for idolatry was curbed. Nor had the Davidic king come. The prophesied time of God's complete redemption through an eternal covenant of peace was still future. Similarly, for Christians today, there are redemptive blessings in the present but the fullness awaits the consummation. Psalm 126 continues:

4 Restore our fortunes, O LORD,
like streams in the desert.
5 Those who sow in tears
will reap with songs of joy.
6 He who goes out weeping,
carrying seed to sow,
will return with songs of joy,
carrying sheaves with him.

The return from exile is not the ultimate fulfilment of Jeremiah's new covenant prediction, but it began with the reconstitution of the remnant of God's people from both Israel and Judah (Jer. 31:31ff., Ezek. 37:15–28).[7] They have been brought back from the dead (Ezek. 37) to again be God's people in God's land under

7 Thus the idea of ten 'lost tribes' is not recognised in Scripture. Note also Acts 26:7; James 1:1.

his Lordship and with a true priesthood. Yet the prophecies of Zechariah (c. 520 BC) show that the goal of the temple building of that time will ultimately lead to a Messianic era when priesthood and kingship will be combined in one person (cf. Ps 110). The day of small things will give way to greater glory through God's Spirit (Zech 4:6).

In Daniel 9:24–27 we find a remarkable prophecy in which the seventy years of captivity in Babylon ended by Cyrus, in this respect the Lord's anointed (Isa. 45:1), complete a cycle but also introduce a further period of '70 sevens'. During this period events which achieve the goal of history will be realised by the true Messiah, the Last Adam.

> 24 "Seventy 'sevens' are decreed for your people and your holy city to finish transgression, to put an end to sin, to atone for wickedness, to bring in everlasting righteousness, to seal up vision and prophecy and to anoint the most holy. 25 "Know and understand this: From the issuing of the decree to restore and rebuild Jerusalem until the Anointed One, the ruler, comes, there will be seven 'sevens,' and sixty-two 'sevens.' It will be rebuilt with streets and a trench, but in times of trouble. 26 After the sixty-two 'sevens,' the Anointed One will be cut off and will have nothing. The people of the ruler who will come will destroy the city and the sanctuary. The end will come like a flood: War will continue until the end, and desolations have been decreed. 27 He will confirm a covenant with many for one 'seven.' In the middle of the 'seven' he will put an end to sacrifice and offering. And on a wing [of the temple] he will set up an abomination that causes desolation, until the end that is decreed is poured out on him."

The passage tells us that the end of the 70 years of exile (Jer. 25:8–14; 29:10) will introduce a new period of 70 units of seven. The sabbath and numerical symbolism in the passage is important, more so that any precise calculation of time.[8] The 70 sevens is a complete and perfect period during which the perfect plan of God will be realised in effective dealing with sin and deliverance from sin's bondage (v24) through Messiah's death (v27 cf Isa. 53) which causes God's covenant to prevail. The end point of the 70 sevens is therefore the eternal sabbath, the goal of history. Notice the 3-fold division:

seven sevens — the city will be rebuilt but no 50th jubilee year follows (Lev. 25:8–13) since true liberty will not follow the rebuilding of Jerusalem; this comes only with the Messiah.

sixty-two sevens — an odd or broken period as if to convey the idea that the period from the rebuilding until the coming of Christ (the first time) is uncertain to us, and a period which, even with what has gone before, is still incomplete.

one seven — the last seven is itself complete, a single seven. Like creation it suggests a new and complete work of God (cf Gen. 1:1ff), but also

8 There are four suggested dates for the beginning of the prophecy: Cyrus' decree concerning Jerusalem and the temple, 538 BC; Darius' decree to restore the temple confirming the decree of Cyrus, 520 BC. (Ezra 5); the decree of Artaxerxes concerning gifts for the temple 458 BC (Ezra 7); the decree for rebuilding the wall, 445 BC (Neh. 2:1ff). While the latter decrees can be seen as based on the first (cf. Ezra 6:14), it is, I think, clear that the work of Cyrus closes the 70 years of the Babylonian captivity and begins the new period of seventy sevens. The day for a year principle is not asserted in the text. Its attraction lies in the ability to calculate a date roughly close to the actual time of Jesus, say from 457 BC to the stoning of Stephen. However, the more one examines the matter the less satisfied with such an approach one becomes, particularly when the sabbath symbolism of the prophecy is appreciated. For a valuable discussion see Meredith G. Kline, 'The Covenant of the Seventieth Week' in J.H. Skilton (ed.), *The Law and the Prophets* (Nutley: Presbyterian & Reformed, 1974), 452–469.

completes the perfect plan of God (70 sevens). In the middle (not at the end) of this seven Jerusalem is destroyed [which it was in AD 70] through the application of the curses of the covenant by the instrumentality of the Romans, leaving three and one half to the end of history. This broken period appears to be a symbol of the Christian dispensation—a period of trial and persecution but also a period that ends in triumph, completing God's perfect plan. [The same period is expressed as 42 months in Rev. 11:2; 13:5 and 1260 days in Rev. 11:3; 12:6.]

So Daniel learns that the city will be rebuilt but eventually be destroyed in order that God's covenant may prevail through Messiah's death so that its full benefits will be realised in the building of the spiritual temple and the establishing of the kingdom which will have no end. The earthly city/temple is not the key: it was always only a symbol of God's presence. Messiah is the key for the future. He is the seed of the woman, the one who defeats the Serpent. Already anticipated as Immanuel, he guides the destiny of Israel in the absence of the king on David's throne, and will come to be personally present with his people.

Kline summarises the meaning of Daniel's 70th week: 'In the course of the climactic seventieth week, *masiah nagid*, the anointed priest-king, would make the covenant prevail both in renewal and judgment. Cut off in death, Messiah would make priestly reconciliation for iniquity, so perfecting sacrifice forever and instituting the new covenant. Then, exercising his royal heavenly rule over all the nations, Messiah in the midst of the seventieth week would send forces of destruction against the Jerusalem temple, so making the old ritual system cease and bringing the old [Mosaic] covenant to its end.'[9]

9 Kline, "The Covenant of the Seventieth Week," 468.

Significantly, the last of the Old Testament books, Malachi (c. 430 BC), speaks to a discouraged and disobedient people of the messenger of God's covenant, the Lord whom you seek, coming suddenly to his temple (3:1). But it will be for judgment as well as for salvation; always there are these two aspects.

7. *Jesus and the New Covenant Reality*

Matthew traces the genealogy of Jesus from Abraham through David (Matt. 1:1), while Luke traces it back to Adam, 'the son of God' (Luke 3:31). Both Mary and Zacharias recognise the coming of Jesus is the fulfilment of the covenant promises to Abraham (Luke 2:55,72–75). John notes that the law came through Moses but grace and truth came into being through Jesus Christ (John 1:17). The idea is not a contrast between what is false and what is true, for indeed the law came through Moses from God, but a contrast between old and new, shadow and reality, and between one who was a messenger and one who was the very embodiment of the message.

The clear portrayal of Jesus as the Last Adam in the temptation should be noted. Jesus' temptation at the beginning of his public ministry is in a setting of social and environmental deprivation—in the desert among wild animals (Mark 1:12–13), not in a garden. It comes from outside of him, from Satan, and it aims to overthrow Jesus' trust in the Father's love and care. But the Last Adam worships and serves the LORD his God according to every word of God. No one is ever able to convict him of sin, and so death should not be his lot. His death is explicable only on the principles of the Father's redemptive purpose: he will yield his son, his only son, whom he loves, Jesus, to bear the sin of others as representative and substitute. He is the Servant of the Lord, the true Passover, the Lamb of God. Here in Christ's sacrifice is the ultimate implication of God's commitment to Abraham to be his God.

In Luke 24:25 the risen Jesus begins at Moses and all the prophets, explaining to the disciples what was said in the Scriptures concerning himself. He also speaks (v.44) of everything written about him in the Law, the Prophets and the Psalms (terms standing for the three great divisions of the Hebrew Bible) having to be fulfilled. Here we have the origin of the Apostolic use of the Old Testament in the early church.

Jesus expressly identifies his sacrifice as 'the new covenant in my blood which is poured out for you' (Luke 22:20), and the New Testament proclaims and applies this reality. Jesus is the Last Adam, the obedient son through whom sinners are redeemed and made the people of God (Rom. 5:12–21). He is the priest-king on the true throne of David exercising his rule so as to put down all his enemies (1 Cor. 15:20–28). His glory will be revealed in the new creation when his task is complete.

The old (Mosaic) covenant is superseded because fulfilled by Jesus (Matt. 5:17). Yet the righteous requirements of the law are fulfilled in Christ's people, for they live according to the Spirit and not the sinful nature (Rom. 8:4). Here again is the internalisation of the law which was to characterise the new covenant referred to by Jeremiah. The moral law of love for God and neighbour, which of old was expressed in the ten commandments rooted in the redemption from slavery in Egypt, is now commended to us by the one who embodied it perfectly, and whose sacrifice as the true

Passover Lamb provides the foundation of the 'new' commandment of love 'as I have loved you' (John 13:24).

Yet the promised accomplishment of the new covenant in a universally holy people is not yet fully realised among the people of God. It still remains that they are not all Israel who are of Israel. The professing people of God are not all regenerate, not all perfectly sanctified.

The ultimate fulfilment of the new covenant is in the final and glorious manifestation of the kingdom of God already established in Jesus. The Book of Revelation reminds us that God will be with his people in an unparalleled way (21:3); there will be no sin in the new creation (21:8,27), no tears, no death (21:4) no curse (22:3). The redeemed will be sons who inherit all this (21:7), servants who serve (22:3), kings who reign (22:5). Conditions in the new creation remind us of Eden, yet far exceed them (22:1ff). The garden becomes a city of light and glory in God's presence forever and ever. God's purpose in creation is realised in a world of love and righteousness. The jubilee climax of the seventieth seven has come, and the endless new creation sabbath is entered upon.

A challenge concludes our review: '...the familiar words of the great Commission of Matthew 28 are cast in the form of an ancient covenant. There is a preamble, "All authority is given to me in heaven and in earth." There is a stipulation, "Go, teach the nations." And there is a promise, "I am with you always."...If we divorce the promise from the stipulation, there is no presence...It is the going church which alone enjoys the promise of the presence of God.'[10]

---

10 Donald Macleod, *A Faith to Live By* (Fearn: Christian Focus, 2002), 131–132.

PART TWO

LITERATURE AND CREEDAL EXPRESSION

In this section a survey is provided introducing leading writers on covenant theology who deal with the covenant of works. The survey is in approximate chronological order and significant creeds or other statements are introduced at the appropriate point. The writers mentioned are representative but include most writers of significance.

There is a bias towards writers associated with the Westminster Assembly with a view to clarifying the significance of statements in the Westminster Confession and Catechisms. Writers from an Arminian, Amyraldian or Antinomian perspective are not featured, but only those who, whatever their ecclesiastical position, were Calvinistic thinkers.

The creed-type documents quoted include the following:

3

COVENANT THINKING BEFORE 1589

Augustine (354–430) had more than once referred to Adam breaking a pre-fall covenant,[1] and the idea is found in other early Christian writings, but systematic development did not occur. Much the same is true of the early Reformation writers. It was recognised that through Adam sin and death had entered the world and that death had passed on all men since all had sinned (Rom. 5:12). However, this was not understood at first to have involved a breaking of a pre-fall covenant in Eden but to have been a natural transmission to Adam's posterity, he being the root of all mankind. In Table 1 are typical creedal statements from 1559/1566 using the language of hereditary evil/disease or propagation but not of imputation. The English Thirty-nine Articles (1563) are to the same effect (see Table 2).

The term covenant can be taken as equivalent to a binding law or unconditional promise, and it is used in this sense by Reformed writers prior to Polanus in 1589. Yet in these writers there is frequently no clear association of the promise of life to Adam if

1 *City of God*, Book XVI, Ch. 27 [NPNF, ed P. Schaff (Peabody: Hendriksen, 1995) Vol.2, 326–327]; *Of Marriage and Concupiscence*, Book II, Ch.24 [NPNF, ed. P. Schaff (Peabody: Hendriksen, 1995), Vol. 5, 292].

obedience is given to God's law, nor is there a clear doctrine of federal headship and the imputation of Adam's sin to his natural posterity. These ideas may be implicit but they are not consciously worked out.

In his 1617 book *A Treatise of Paradise*, Protestant convert from Rome, **John Salkeld** (1576–1660), poses the question, 'Whether it was necessary that there should be made a covenant between God and man, that so original sin might descend to the posterity of Adam.' He asserts that Ambrosius Catharinus Pilitus (1483–1553), the Roman Catholic controversialist, held such a pact to be necessary, and that it was in the words of Genesis 2:17, whereas Dominic Soto (1494–1560) regarded admission of such a pact as frivolous, *De natura et gracia* (Venice 1547) Chapter 10.[2] Both these Roman Catholic theologians were of note in their time and both participated in the Council of Trent. However, while strongly advocating the imputation of Adam's sin to his posterity, Catharinus rejected the transmission of a corrupt nature, which Trent and Protestants alike affirmed.[3]

Although covenant doctrine can be traced in an undeveloped state in the 1520s and 1530s in writings of Swiss Reformers such as Huldrych Zwingli (1484–1531), Johannes Oecolampadius (1482–1531) and Heinrich Bullinger (1504–75), and also in John Calvin (1509–64), clarity is attained only later in the 16th century.

---

2 John Salkeld, *A Treatise of Paradise* (London: N Butter, 1617), 302.

3 For discussion see William Cunningham, *The Reformers and the Theology of the Reformation* [1862] (London: Banner of Truth, 1967), 377ff. Catharinus wrote a short work on original sin and justification in *Speculum haereticorum* (Lyons 1541).

TABLE 1[4]

FRENCH CONFESSION 1559	SCOTS CONFESSION 1560	BELGIC CONFESSION 1561	2ND HELVETIC CONFESSION 1566
Article 9: We believe that man was created pure and perfect in the image of God, and that by his own guilt he fell from the grace (de la grâce) which he received, and is thus alienated from God, the fountain of justice and of all good, so that his nature is totally corrupt... **Article 10:** We believe that all the posterity of Adam is in bondage to original sin, which is an hereditary evil, and not an imitation merely, as was declared by the Pelagians, whom we detest in their errors. And we consider that it is not necessary to inquire how sin was conveyed from one man to another, for what God had given Adam was not for him alone, but for his posterity; and thus in his person we have been deprived of all good things, and have fallen with him into a state of Sin and misery..	**Chapter 2:** We confess and acknowledge that our God has created man, i.e., our first father, Adam, after his own image and likeness, to whom he gave wisdom, lordship, justice, free will, and self-consciousness, so that in the whole nature of man no imperfection could be found. From this dignity and perfection man and woman both fell... **Chapter 3:** By this transgression, commonly known as original sin, the image of God was utterly defaced in man , and he and his children became by nature hostile to God, slaves to Satan, and servants to sin. And thus everlasting death has had, and shall have, power and dominion over all who have not been, are not, or shall not be reborn from above....	**Article 14:** We believe that God created man out of the earth and formed him after his own image and likeness, good, righteous and holy, perfect in all things, capable in all things to will agreeably to the will of God.... **Article 15:** We believe that, through the disobedience of Adam, original sin is extended to all mankind; which is a corruption of the whole nature, and an hereditary disease, wherewith infants themselves are affected even in their mother's womb, and which produces in man all sorts of sin, being in him as a root of it...	**Chapter 8:** *THE FALL OF MAN.* In the beginning man was made according to the image of God, in righteousness and true holiness, good and upright. But when at the instigation of the serpent and by his own fault he abandoned goodness and righteousness, he became subject to sin, death and various calamities. And what he became by the fall, that is, subject to sin, death and various calamities, so are all those who have descended from him. *SIN.* By sin we understand that innate corruption of man which has been derived or propagated in us all from our first parents, by which we, immersed in perverse desires and averse to all good, are inclined to all evil...

4 Text of **French Confession** in English in P. & D.S. Schaff (eds.), *Creeds of Christendom* (New York: Harper & Row, 1931), Vol. 3, 265. **Scots Confession** text in G.D.Henderson (ed), *The Scots Confession 1560* (Edinburgh: St Andrew Press, 1960). The 1619 text of the **Belgic Confession** approved by the Synod of Dordt is in French and English in Schaff, *Creeds of Christendom*, 3.398 but includes the addition 'mud of the' before 'earth' and omits 'perfect in all things'. Both changes apparently were made in the interest of avoiding an exaggerated view of the original perfection of Adam, and

German born **Wolfgang Musculus** (1497–1563), Professor at Bern from 1549, published his *Loci Communes* about 1555. and it was translated into English in 1563. Musculus is aware of what he thinks obvious:, that covenant means 'a bargain or agreement' which is 'confirmed by an oath' and 'made void by death' and thus is distinguished from a testament which is ratified on the death of the testator. He writes, 'the covenant of God is of two sorts. One is general and the other is special and everlasting. The general covenant is that which he made with the whole frame of the earth and all that dwelleth therein, as well beasts as men, with the day also and the night, winter and summer, cold and heat, seed time and harvest.' After citing God's promise to Noah in Genesis 9:9–11,15b and the words of Jeremiah 33:20ff, he adds:

> 'This covenant is general, because it concerneth the whole world: it may be called earthly and temporal, because it doth touch the steadfastness of earthly matters, as appeareth by the very words: and it endureth no longer than the standing of this world, that once perished.'[5]

This covenant of preservation, as we might call it, is clearly of importance to Musculus, but it is post-fall, serves the interests of

---

were for substance introduced already by the Synod of Antwerp in 1566. Cf. C. Vonk, *De voorzeide leer, IIIa: De Nederlandse Geloofsbelijdenis art. 1–21 en 25–26 [The aforesaid doctrine, IIIa: The Belgic Confession, articles 1–21 and 25–26],* (Barendrecht: Barendrecht, 1955) 341–342; also J.N. Bakhuizen van den Brink, *De Nederlandse belijdenisgeschriften in authentieke teksten met inleiding en tekstvergelijkingen, [The Dutch confessions in authentic texts with introduction and comparison of texts]* (Amsterdam: Bolland, second edition 1976) 93–94. I record my appreciation to the Revd Rutger ter Beek of Meidoornveld, The Netherlands for these references and for translation assistance. The **Second Helvetic Confession** text is in Arthur C. Cochrane, *Reformed Confessions of the 16th Century* (Westminster Press, 1966), 235.

5 Wolfgang Musculus, *Loci Communes Sacrae Theologiae* (?Bern, 1555) translated by John Man of Oxford as *Common Places of Christian Religion* (London, 1563), 120–121.

redemption and is not tied to a specific moral claim on Adam. There is no covenant of works in this general covenant. The special and everlasting covenant Musculus identifies with the Abrahamic covenant (Gen. 17).

The authors of the great Heidelberg Catechism (1562), **Zachary Ursinus** (1534–83) and **Caspar Olevianus** (1536–87), were important in the development of covenant thinking. Olevianus speaks of a 'covenant of creation' [*foedus creationis*], being the obligation of obedience inherent in the human's status as God's image-bearer, hence the synonyms he uses—covenant of nature and covenant of law. However, he does not attach to it the promise of life if obedience is given to the obligation (or to the specific command in Paradise), nor does he recognise Adam's representative headship and the imputation of Adam's sin to his posterity.[6]

As early as 1562 Ursinus spoke of a 'covenant of nature' [*foedus naturale*] in reference to the law of nature including the moral law given at creation and repeated at Sinai, but he does not develop this further either.[7]

However, Ursinus defines law in a way requiring a reward for obedience:

> 'A Law in general is a sentence commanding that which is honest, and binding the reasonable creature to obedience, with a promise of reward

6 L.D. Bierma, *German Calvinism in the Confessional Age* (Grand Rapids: Baker, 1996), 112–120. For a different assessment in more traditional terms see R. Scott Clark, *The Substance of the Covenant: Caspar Olevian on the Double Benefit of Christ* (Grand Rapids: Reformation Heritage, 2005).

7 Bierma, *German Calvinism*, 58–59.

> if that obedience be performed, and threatening of punishment, if it be violated.'[8]

This seems in contrast to Calvin who rejects any reward prior to Moses '*since there was no covenant*'.[9] So it can be said that Ursinus has in essence a two-covenant structure in his theology. This is confirmed in his *Summa theologiae*, the Major catechism written about the end of 1561:

> ***Q.10: What does the divine law teach?***
>
> The sort of covenant which God began with man, in creation; by which man should have carried himself in serving God; and what God would require from him after beginning with him a new covenant of grace; that is, how and for what [end] man was created by God; and to what state he might be restored; and by which covenant one who has been reconciled to God ought to arrange his life.
>
> ***Q.36: What distinguishes law and gospel?***
>
> The law contains a covenant of nature begun by God with men in creation, that is, it is a natural sign to men, and it requires of us perfect obedience toward God. It promises eternal life to those keeping it, and threatens eternal punishment to those not keeping it. In fact, the gospel contains a covenant of grace, that is, one known not at all under nature. This covenant declares to us fulfilment of its righteousness in Christ, which

8 Zachary Ursinus, *A Collection of Certain Learned Discourses* translated from the Latin text of David Pareus by I.H. (London: J. Broome, 1600), 256 (italics in original).

9 John Calvin, *The Epistles of Paul to the Galatians, Ephesians, Philippians and Colossians* [1548] translated by T.H.L.Parker (Edinburgh: Oliver and Boyd, 1965), 59 [on Gal 3:17].

> the law requires, and our restoration through Christ's Spirit. To those who believe in him, it freely promises eternal life for Christ's sake.[10]

The first known British usage of the term 'covenant' in relation to Adam is in the translation of Hosea 6:7 in the first printed English Bible, that by Coverdale, in 1535: 'But even like as Adam did, so have they broken my covenant...' with a text reference to Genesis 3 in the margin.[11] The gifted young Englishman **Dudley Fenner** (c. 1558–87), employs the expression 'covenant of works' to describe the covenant with Israel but does not apply it to the pre-fall relationship.[12]

Fenner's mentor, **Thomas Cartwright** (1535–1603), was deprived of his position at Cambridge because of non-conformity, lived on the Continent 1573–85 and was imprisoned in England 1590–92. He produced a Catechism published first in 1604. In it Cartwright uses the term 'covenant of works' but he does not carry it back to Eden in as many words, nor does he speak clearly of imputation. In his Catechism the covenant of works follows the fall:

---

10 The English translation is cited from R. Scott Clark and Joel Beeke, 'Ursinus, Oxford and the Westminster Divines' in J. Ligon Duncan et al (eds.), *The Westminster Confession into the 21st Century: Essays in Remembrance of the 350th Anniversary of the Westminster Confession of Faith*, Vol 2 (Fearn: Mentor, 2004). 1–32.

11 Covenant theologians had no uniform view of Hosea 6:7 although Muller notes that virtually all patristic and medieval commentators were agreed that the text referred to the breaking of a pre-fall covenant with God by Adam. The best surveys are B.B.Warfield, *Selected Shorter Writings Vol 1* (Grand Rapids: Baker, 2003), 116–129 who prefers 'like Adam'; also Richard A. Muller, *Post Reformation Reformed Dogmatics* Vol.2 (Grand Rapids, Baker, 2003), 436–441.

12 In his *Sacra Theologia* (London 1585); cf. Michael McGiffert, 'From Moses to Adam: The Making of the Covenant of works' in *The Sixteeth Century Journal*, XIX. 2 (Summer 1988), 136ff.

> [Q34] ***What is that which God hath ordained for the repair of man?*** His word.
>
> [Q37] ***What are the parts of the word?*** The law and [the] gracious promise: otherwise called the Covenant of works, and the Covenant of grace which from the coming of Christ is called the Gospel.
>
> [Q38] ***What doeth the Law (containing the Covenant of works) crave of us?*** All such duties as were required of Adam in his innocency, and all such as are required since by reason of his fall, with reward of life everlasting to the doers of them, and curses to him that doeth them not.[13]

William Perkins (1558–1602), the very widely read Cambridge Puritan, says that the word of God sets down two covenants: one legal the other evangelical,[14] and he describes the covenant of works as 'God's covenant, made with condition of perfect obedience, and is expressed in the moral Law.' But he is thinking of the law of Moses, of which the ten commandments are an abridgement.[15] Although Perkins says 'the law was in nature by creation', he does not use the term covenant of works for the pre-Mosaic period or for the creation relationship.

Similarly, in 1589 a friend of Dudley Fenner, apparently Sir **Henry Finch** (1558–1625),[16] published anonymously a brief work entitled *The Sacred Doctrine of Divinitie Gathered Out of the Worde*

13 Cartwright's Catechism follows page 372 in J.Dod and R Cleaver, *A Plaine and familiar Exposition of the Ten Commandments, with a methodical Short Catechism, containing briefly all the principall grounds of Christian Religion* (London: Thomas Man, 1604). It reached a 16th edition by 1625. The citation is from (unnumbered) page 4 in the 1604 edition. Cartwright's *A Treatise of Christian Religion* (London: Thomas Man, 1616), 74 is to the same effect.

14 William Perkins, *A Reformed Catholike* [1597] in *Works* (London 1605), 692.

15 William Perkins, *The Golden Chaine*, [1591] in *Works* (1605), 82–83.

16 William Perkins, *A Commentarie upon the Epistle of the Galatians* (London, 2nd ed., 1592), 347 [on Gal 4:24–25].

of God.[17] In it he writes of two kinds of righteousness—our own or from another.

> 'The first, requiring righteousness from ourselves, or by our own works, and propounding life everlasting if we do it, is called the Law, or the covenant of works, Rom 10:5; Gal 3:12. The other, sending us to Christ, and propounding life everlasting through him, if we believe in him, is called the covenant of grace, Rom 10:4; Gal 3:13–14.'[18]

This book was reprinted in a somewhat revised form in 1613 in which Chapter XVI is titled The Covenant of Works. It follows the treatment of the commandments and consists of four sentences thus:

> Righteousness thus set forth in his several parts and branches, has of God's free goodness a reward belonging to it, (whereupon the same [is] called the Law, or covenant of works;) as contrariwise a punishment in his Justice to those that sin against it: both more or less, as the righteousness or sin abounds. The reward is blessedness, which is the having of all things that make the creature happy, and stands in the fruition of God alone, or, from thence coming, conjunction and communion with him. Conjunction is the enjoying of his personal presence. Communion is a participation (in some sort) of his blessedness both in kingdom power and glory.[19]

---

17 Henry Finch, *The Sacred Doctrine of Divinitie Gathered Out of the Worde of God* (Middelburg: Richard Schilders). The title page gives the date as 1599 but the preface is dated 1 January 1589 and the content of the preface in its references to Fenner confirms the earlier date is the correct one. The Preface refers to a similar work by Fenner, presumably his *Grounds of Religion Set Down in Question and Answer* (Middelburg, 1587), which I have not inspected.

18 Henry Finch, *The Sacred Doctrine of Divinitie* (Middelburg: Richard Schilders), 30.

19 Henry Finch, *The Sacred Doctrine of Divinitie* (London: Felix Kyngston, 1613), 9.

If the covenant of works can equate to the natural relation in creation, it is also possible to not use the term but describe the relationship in equivalent terms. **William Bucanus**, Professor of Theology at Lausanne from 1591 to his death in 1603, does not use the term covenant of works for God's relationship with Adam, and appears to think of the relationship as one of law as distinct from covenant. He also uses the term covenant for 'that one perpetual covenant of God, whereby God binds himself to give salvation to all those who believe in Christ'.[20] Yet he draws the conclusions typical of those who speak specifically of a post-creation, pre-fall covenant with Adam—representative headship, the imputation of Adam's sin to his posterity,[21] as well as the promise of heavenly life.[22] He thus represents a transition in covenant thought which is really already implicit in men like Cartwright. Bucanus can also be seen as the earliest example of a position like that of the 20th century Reformed theologian, John Murray.

---

20 William Bucanus, *Institutiones Theologicae* (Bremen 1605) translated by Robert Hill as *Institutions of Christian Religion* (London 1606), 215.

21 William Bucanus, *Institutions of Christian Religion*, 162.

22 William Bucanus, *Institutions of Christian Religion*, 111.

4

A POST-CREATION, PRE-FALL COVENANT

From the late 1580s the covenant concept is increasingly applied to the relationship with Adam established after creation as recorded in Genesis 2:16–17, and thus to an agreement between parties involving promises upon the filling of specified conditions, the covenant of works, as it was commonly called.

Amandus Polanus (1561–1610), Professor of Divinity at Basel and a voluminous writer, published his Latin work *Partitiones Theologicæ* at Basel in 1589. A second edition was issued in 1590 and a further printing in London in 1591. It was translated into English in 1595 with subsequent printings in 1597, 1600 and 1608. This appears to be the earliest clear example in the literature in which a post-creation, pre-fall covenant of works with Adam is identified,[1] although it is not discussed in detail.

1 Since reading Polanus, I have had access to N.Deimer's work *Het Scheppingsverbond met Adam (het verbond der werken) bij de theologen der 16th, 17th en 18th eeuw in Zwitserland, Duitschland, Nederland en Engeland* [*The Creation Covenant with Adam (the Covenant of Works): theologians of the 16th, 17th and 18th centuries in Switzerland, Germany, The Netherlands and England*] (Kampen: Kok, 1935) in which in a brief survey he states: "Polanus was the first theologian to speak of 'the covenant of works'." I record my debt to Rev R.C. Janssen of Nagele, The Netherlands for this reference and the translation. So also Karl Barth, *Church Dogmatics* IV/1 (Edinburgh: T & T Clark, 1956), 59. Cf. Also Mark McGiffert,

As essentially an outline of Polanus' theology, the book was intended to lead on to a greater elaboration in his *Syntagma Theologicæ Christianæ* published in 1609/10.[2]

In Britain, *Tractatus De Vocatione Efficaci* (Edinburgh 1597) by **Robert Rollock** (1555–99) includes the earliest well-formed statement identifying a pre-fall covenant with Adam. Rollock (1555–99) was Principal and Professor of Theology at Edinburgh University. Rollock goes beyond Olevianus in connecting the covenant of works to the promise of life, and his presentation is more substantial than that of Polanus. His book was translated into English in 1603. Rollock holds that 'all the word of God pertains to some covenant' adding 'for God speaks nothing to man without the covenant'. His definition is as follows: 'The covenant of God generally is a promise under some certain condition. And it is twofold: the first is the covenant of works; the second is the covenant of grace....'[3]

John Ball (1585–1640) was one of the fathers of English Presbyterianism. He graduated MA from St Mary's Hall Oxford, and was ordained in 1610. He was more than once imprisoned for nonconformity. He spent his life in poverty caring for a small church in Staffordshire. In 1615 he issued anonymously a catechism with commentary entitled *A short treatise: contayning all the principall grounds of Christian Religion. By way of Questions and Answers,* very

"From Moses to Adam," 151; in the text McGiffert dates Polanus' teaching from 1595, overlooking that the original Latin edition was 1589; the slip is perpetuated in D.N.J.Poole, *Stages of Religious Faith in the Classical Reformation Tradition* (Lewiston: Mellon, 1995) 171, 192.

2 Cf. Richard A. Muller, *God, Creation and Providence in the Thought of Jacob Arminius* (Grand Rapids: Baker, 1991), 49.

3 Robert Rollock, *A Treatise of God's Effectual Calling,* trans. Henry Holland (London: T. Man, 1603), 6. He had used the two-fold phrase in 1596 in his Latin work *Quaestiones and Responsiones.*

profitable for all men, but especially for Householders. It reached a 4th impression in 1624 and an 11th in 1637. The catechism was published separately at some point, the 13th edition being issued in 1630 and the 34th in 1653. These were very popular and influential works. Ball thinks of God making a promise to the man on condition of obedience to a special command by which he and his posterity would continue in the good state in which he had been created. He writes:

> 'All mankind were created good in Adam, as other creatures were in their kind, and God did enter into covenant with our first parents as they were the root of all their posterity: so that what they had actually promised to them, we had promised to us also in them.'[4] 'Adam was not a private person, but the common parent of us all; and as he received integrity for himself and us, so he lost it for himself and us.'[5]

The immediate service to theology of the two covenants approach was the clear recognition of the imputation of Adam's sin to his natural posterity. This was expressed in the *Irish Articles* of 1615 (drafted by James Ussher) and the draft revision of the *Thirty-nine Articles* in 1643, in both in a way which does not distinguish the two pre-fall states (see Table 2), and in the *Westminster Confession* of 1646 in a way which does. In 1644, the *Reformed Synod of Charenton*, France, condemned the view of Josue de la Place which restricted 'the nature of Sin to the sole Hereditary Corruption of Adam's posterity, to the exclusion of the Imputation of that first Sin by which he fell'. It required all teachers to acknowledge 'the

4 John Ball, *A short treatise* (London: Thomas Pauier, 1624), 67.
5 John Ball, *A short treatise*, 70.

common received opinion of the Protestant Churches' on this point,[6] ie. imputation as well as corruption of nature.

William Perkins' famous student, **William Ames** (1576–1633) taught a covenant of works with Adam in a clear if modest way. He affirmed in his *The Marrow of Theology* (1623) the addition of a positive command to the law of nature. It involved 'a promise of continuing animal life, a later exaltation to spiritual life, and a threat of bodily death.' He described it as 'the law of God or his covenant with man in the creation'.[7] Ames had been forced out of England in 1610 and spent his remaining years in the Netherlands. He was consultant to the moderator of the Synod of Dordt in 1619 and taught at Franeker 1622–32. Only Ames' death prevented his move to New England where, nevertheless, his writings were enormously influential at Harvard and Yale for 50 years or more.

Johannes Wollebius (1586–1629), who studied under Polanus, was Old Testament Professor at Basel from 1618. He wrote similarly: 'God's covenant with man is twofold, a covenant of works and one of grace: the first before the fall, and the second after it.'[8]

From this date there is really no point adducing further examples as Covenant Theology on the two-covenant scheme was now the accepted orientation of Reformed thought. Notes on some of the significant writers adhering to this position who will be quoted later will be given at this point.

---

6 B.G.Armstrong, *Calvin and the Amyraut Heresy* (Wisconsin,1969), 104–105.

7 William Ames, *Medulla Theologica* (Amsterdam, 1623) translated by J.D.Eusden as *The Marrow of Theology* (Durham, NC: Labyrinth Press, 1983), I. X. 31,32 (p.113).

8 Cf. Johannes Wollebius, *Compendium Theologiae Christianae* (Basel 1626), translation by J.W.Beardslee (ed.), *Reformed Dogmatics* (Grand Rapids: Baker, 1977), 64.

TABLE 2[9]

ENGLISH THIRTY-NINE ARTICLES, 1563	IRISH ARTICLES, 1615	DRAFT REVISION OF THIRTY-NINE ARTICLES, 1643
Article 9: Original sin standeth not in the following of Adam (as the Pelagians do vainly talk), but it is the fault and corruption of the nature of every man that naturally is engendered of the offspring of Adam, whereby man is very far gone from original righteousness, and is of his own nature inclined to evil, so that the flesh lusteth always contrary to the Spirit; and therefore in every person born into this world, it deserveth God's wrath and damnation. And this infection of nature doth remain, yea in them that are regenerate, whereby the lust of the flesh, called in Greek, φρονεμα σαρκοσ which some do expound the wisdom, some sensuality, some the affection, some the desire of the flesh, is not subject to the law of God...	**Article 21**: Man being at the beginning created according to the image of God (which consisted especially in the wisdom of his mind and the true holiness of his free will), had the covenant of the law ingrafted in his heart, whereby God did promise unto him everlasting life upon condition that he performed entire and perfect obedience unto his Commandments, according to that measure of strength wherewith he was endued in his creation, and threatened death unto him if he did not perform the same. **Article 22:** By one man sin entered the world, and death by sin; and so death went over all men, forasmuch as all have sinned. **Article 23***:* Original sin standeth not in the imitation of Adam (as the Pelagians dream), but is the fault and corruption of every person that naturally is engendered and propagated from Adam...	**Article 9**: Original sin standeth not in the following of Adam as the Pelagians do vainly talk: but together with his first sin imputed, it is the fault and corruption of the nature of every man that naturally is propagated from Adam; whereby man is wholly deprived of original righteousness, and is of his own nature inclined only to evil. So that the lust of the flesh, called φρονεμα σαρκοσ, which some do expound the wisdom, some sensuality, some the affection, some the desire of the flesh, is not subject to the law of God; and therefore in every person born into this world it deserveth God's wrath and condemnation. And this infection of nature doth remain, yea, in them that are regenerate, whereby the flesh lusteth always contrary to the Spirit.

9 The English text of the **Thirty-nine Articles** is that approved in 1571, but with modern spelling, and on Article 9 has no significant difference from the original Latin text of 1563; cf. Schaff, *Creeds of Christendom,* 3.493. The **Irish Articles** is in Schaff, *Creeds of Christendom*, 3.530. The draft revision of the **Thirty-nine Articles** is in Daniel Neal, *The History of the Puritans* (London: William Baynes & Son, 1822) v.5, Appendix VII, p. viii.

For completeness of reference to Reformed Confessions, one could note that the Confession of the Eastern Orthodox Patriarch of Constantinople, **Cyril Lucaris** (1572–1638), written in March 1629, does not refer to the covenant, although as a Confession it is undoubtedly to be classified as Reformed. Cyril writes in Chapter 6:

> 'We believe that the first man created by God fell in Paradise, because he neglected the commandment of God and yielded to the deceitful counsel of the serpent. From thence sprung up original sin to his posterity, so that no man is born according to the flesh who does not bear this burden and feel the fruits of it in his life.'[10]

In Britain covenant thought was general. Dr **John Preston** (1587–1628) was a powerful preacher at Lincoln's Inn from 1622 and then Master of Emmanuel College, Cambridge and Chaplain to the King. Fourteen of his sermons were published as *The New Covenant* in 1629, and there were at least seven further printings to 1640.[11]

About 1628/30 The *Summe of Sacred Divinitie* by Bishop **John Downame** was published. The 1589/1613 volume referred to on page 58f was included as an introductory outline to Downame's own very substantial treatment.[12] Downame's version of Chapter XVI referred to earlier is as follows:

---

10 Translated by Dennis Bratcher, Christian Resource Institute, Oklahoma, USA.

11 For the covenant of works see John Preston, *The New Covenant* (London 1629), 317.

12 Cf. Richard A. Muller, 'Covenant and Conscience in English Reformed Theology' in *Westminster Theological Journal* XLII.2 (Spring 1980), 312–3.

> 'With the creatures, who are thus to do his Will, it hath pleased God to make a Covenant, which is called the Covenant of Works: A Covenant of Life, to the doers; of Death, unto Transgressors: Both more, or less, as the Righteousness or Sin aboundeth. Life is a continual progress in Holiness and Happiness. Death is a Sinful and Cursed Estate. Sinful, in Darkness, and a total corruption of the whole strength of Nature, unto all unrighteousness. Cursed, in the Wrath of God, and all the evil that cometh of it; contrary to the former, Conjunction and Communion with him.'[13]

Edward Leigh (1602–71) graduated MA from Magdalen Hall, Oxford in 1623 and afterwards studied law. A scholarly layman, he compiled works on the meaning of the Hebrew and Greek words of the Bible. He was member for Stafford 1644–48, but was expelled by the Parliament for voting that the King Charles' concessions were satisfactory. The relevant book for our purposes is in fact his first, *A Treatise of the Divine Promises* (1633).

In the *Staten Vertaling* Dutch Bible commissioned by the States-General and published in 1637, the following appears as one of four introductory items preceding the New Testament, and shows the general prevalence of the teaching on the covenant of works at that time.

> The word 'Testament' is a Latin word [*Testamentum*]. It translates the Greek word *Diatheke*, which the Greek Translators used to express the Hebrew word *Berith*, meaning 'Covenant.' Thereby is to be understood the Covenant itself which God made with man[kind] in order, under certain conditions, to give him everlasting life. That Covenant is twofold – the Old and the New. The Old is that which God made with the first man before the fall, in

13 John Downame, *The Summe of Sacred Divinitie First Briefly and Methodically Propounded and then More Largly and Cleerly Handled and Explained* (London: Geo Hodges, n.d) unpaginated.

> which everlasting life was promised on condition of an altogether perfect obedience and keeping of the Law. Therefore it is called the Covenant of the Law, which God [later] once again held forth to the Israelites.... Because this condition has been transgressed with all men, and cannot now be fulfilled by any man [save Jesus], they must seek their salvation in another Covenant. That is called New. It consists of God foreordaining His Son as a Mediator. He promises everlasting life, on condition that we trust in Him. It is called the Covenant of Grace. Because of its various administrations to mankind, it is also called Old and New. The Old is the administration of that Covenant before the coming of the Mediator who was promised to Abraham and his descendants from his seed – and portrayed by many kind of ceremonies described by Moses. The New is the administration of that same Covenant – after the Son of God and Mediator of that Covenant came in the flesh and effected the reconciliation of man with God. These two Covenants are indeed one and the same as regards their essence—for both promise forgiveness of sins and salvation and everlasting life, on the condition that one trust the Mediator. But they are distinguished in respect of the administration of both. The New is much clearer, is without illustrations, and extends itself to all nations.[14]

George Walker (c. 1581–1651) was educated at Cambridge and was rector of St John the Evangelist in Watling Street, London from 1614. He was censured by Archbishop Laud in 1635 and

14 Text translated from page 5 of the facsimile of the 1637 edition (Kampen: Kok, 1915) by Emeritus-Professor F. Nigel Lee, Brisbane, Australia, July 2002. The notes in the *Staten-Vertaling* were authored by Johannes Bogerman (Professor of Theology at Franeker), Willem Baudartius (the Dordt Synod's Old Testament translator), Gerson Bucerus (Hebrew and History Scholar of Leiden), Antonius Thisius (Professor of Theology at Harderwijk), Jacob Roland (First Assessor at the Synod of Dordt), Herman Faukelius of Middelburg, Petrus Cornelius of Enkhuizen, Festus Hommius (Professor of Homiletics and Dogmatics at Leiden), Antonius Walaeus (Professor of Greek & Philosophy at Middelburg) and Jodocus Hoingius (Rector of Harderwijk).

imprisoned for his preaching 1638–41. In 1640 his *The Manifold Wisdome of God* was published without his express permission and was reprinted the following year. The Preface indicates the book was written 24 years before (ie. 1616) and had circulated in manuscript. Walker was a member of the Westminster Assembly.

5

WESTMINSTER PERIOD, 1643–47

Johannes Cloppenburg (1592–1652), who taught at Harderwijk from 1640 and at Franeker from 1644, issued his work on the Covenant in 1643.[1] Cloppenburg distinguishes the natural state of Adam and the subsequent covenant of works in the usual way.

Important also for discussions on the role of the law for the Christian is Dr **Tobias Crisp** (1600–43), a wealthy rector in Wiltshire. His *Christ Alone Exalted* (1643), a collection of sermons published after his death, was influential. He had been a strong Arminian and over-reacted into a somewhat antinomian position, although his own life was upright. Crisp was not as antinomian as some of his followers.

The **First London Confession** of the English Baptists (1644) is non-specific on imputation or any covenant with Adam or Moses, but has several references to the new covenant. It was largely derived from the Separatist Confession of 1596.

The modest work of **James Ussher** (1580–1656) called *The Principles of Christian Religion Summarily set downe according to the word of God: together with a breife Epitome of the Bodie of*

1 Johannes Cloppenburg, *Disputationes de foedere Dei et testamento veteri et novo* (Basel 1643).

Divinitie was issued in 1645. It consists of two catechisms: (1) The Principles of Christian Religion (pages 1–42); and (2) The Method of the Doctrine of Christian Religion (pages 45–124). The latter claims to be an expansion of some points in the former. Ussher's treatment is brief and unremarkable, with his comments in the Method following his *Irish Articles* of 1615 closely

In the year 1645 Simeon Ashe issued posthumously the major work by the **John Ball** mentioned earlier, *A Treatise on the Covenant of Grace*, with a recommendation based on the reputation of the author by five members[2] of the Westminster Assembly, which was dealing with the covenant at that time.[3] Three other works worthy of mention also appeared in this important year.

The first was called *A Body of Divinitie or the Summe and Substance of Christian Religion Catechistically Handled, Propounded and Explained by Way of Question and Answer collected long since out of Sundry Authors and reduced unto one common method.* It had a preface by Bishop John Downame in which he said the work had been written 'above twenty years since' and the title page ascribed it to James Ussher. There was a second printing in 1647, and others in 1648, 1649, 1653, 1658, 1670, 1677 and 1702 [also 1841] so this substantial volume was popular. However, Ussher claimed that he was not the author as such. He had made a compilation 'out of Mr Cartwright's catechism and Mr [Samuel] Crooke's[4] and some other English Divines...as a kind of common place book...in divers

2 They were Edward Reynolds, Thomas Hill, Daniel Cawdrey, Anthony Burgess and Edmund Calamy. The 'To the Reader' by Ashe is dated 12 June 1645.

3 The Second Committee was instructed 16 July 1645, report was given 9 October, and it was debated several times until 23 December 1645. The work was reviewed and concluded 25 June 1646, with Scripture proofs settled 5 February 1647.

4 Samuel Crooke (1575–1649) published his popular *Guide to True Blessedness* in 1613; it reached a 6th edition in 1640.

places dissonant from my own judgment'. It had been circulated in single sheets and much of what was printed was defective, Ussher claimed.[5]

The second book was called *The True Bounds of Christian Freedom* by **Samuel Bolton**, Master of Christ's College, and was a discussion of the law and the Christian. In it he deals with the relationship of the Mosaic covenant to the covenants of works and of grace. The preface is dated 23 April 1645.[6]

'E.F.' published the first edition of *The Marrow of Moderne Divinitie*. It was cast in the form of a discussion between four characters on issues related to the law and free grace. It was expanded in the second edition 1646, and a second part was added in 1649. It was often reprinted, particularly from 1726 with important notes added by Thomas Boston (1676–1732). 'E.F.' was not, as was later supposed, Edward Fisher of Brasenose College, Oxford, but another **Edward Fisher,** an intelligent Presbyterian layman and member of the Guild of Barber-surgeons in London.[7]

Anthony Burgess (c.1608–1664) was the son of a schoolmaster in Watford, Hartfordshire, was educated at Cambridge and became a fellow of Emmanuel College. Later he pastored a church in Warwickshire, and was a member of the Westminster Assembly. A

5 Letter dated 13 May 1645 in *The Whole Works of James Ussher Vol. 1* (Dublin 1847–64), 249 (life by C.R. Elrington). B.G.Armstrong, *Calvin and the Amyraut Heresy*, 141, unlike many writers, rejects Ussher's authorship, but then wrongly ascribes it to John Downame.

6 The most convenient edition is that by the Banner of Truth Trust in 1964 but does not includes the translation of John Cameron's Theses which in the original forms pages 353–401. Bolton was appointed to the Assembly of Divines after Jeremiah Burroughs' death in November 1646.

7 William Vandoodewaard, *The Marrow Controversy and Seceder Tradition* (Grand Rapids: Reformation Heritage, 2011), 10–22 provides the best summary of the authorship question.

very capable man, he was ejected for non-conformity in 1662 and retired to Tamworth in Staffordshire. His first major work (1646, 2nd edition 1647) was *Vindiciae Legis, or, A Vindication of the Moral Law and the Covenants.* It consisted of 29 lectures against the antinomian errors of the time, and was published at the request of Sion College, the meeting place of Presbyterian ministers in London.

Peter Bulkeley (1583–1659), like John Cotton, a Cambridge-educated Puritan who left for New England in the 1630s, issued the first edition of *The Gospel-Covenant; or The Covenant of Grace Opened* in 1646. An enlarged edition was published in London in 1651. Essentially this is the fruit of preaching in the church at Concord from where Bulkeley exercised a very influential ministry.

Edmund Calamy (1600–66), the popular and leading Presbyterian minister in London, and a member of the Westminster Assembly, was not happy with some of Burgess' words about the Mosaic covenant. Indeed, he provides evidence of the variety of ways in which men spoke of the covenants in a 30 page pamphlet published early in 1646.[8] In this little known work, *Two solemne Covenants Made Between God and Man*, Calamy comments on the diversity of opinion on the covenants, particularly how the covenant with Moses fitted in:

> "There be several opinions about the Covenant of Works, and the Covenant of grace, to the great disturbance of many Christians; [1.] some hold that

8 Edmund Calamy, *Two solemne Covenants made betweene God and Man: viz. The Covenants of Workes, And the Covenant of Grace* (London: Thomas Banks, 1647), 1. The actual date of publication is Feb 1st, 1646/7 - (Old Style/New Style). The English, at this time, marked the new year on Mary Day (March 25th) and not January 1st. I had access to a copy of this pamphlet through the kindness of Dr. Chad Van Dixhoorn, who was then pursuing doctoral research in the materials of the Westminster Assembly at Cambridge, England.

there be four Covenants, two of Works and two of Grace; the two first, one with *Adam* before the fall, and the other with *Israel* at their return out of *Egypt*, and the Covenants of Grace the first to *Abraham*, and the other at the incarnation of Jesus Christ; this *Mr Sympson*[9] affirmed before a Committee of the Assembly of Divines in my hearing.

2. Others hold that there are but three Covenants, the first with *Adam*, the second with *Israel* at their going out of *Egypt*, and a third with Jesus Christ, the two first of Works and the last of Grace, and this *Mr Burroughs*[10] delivered in his Exposition Sermon in *Cornhill* in my hearing.

3. Others hold that there is [sic] but two Covenants, the one of Works and the other of Grace; yet the first they hold was made with Israel at Mount Sinai, and no Covenant of Works before that, and now is vanished away, and the other a Covenant of grace yet not made until the death of Christ the testator, and this is affirmed by James Pope, in a [recently published] book entitled *The unveiling of Antichrist.*

4. Others hold that the Law at Mount Sinai was a covenant of grace, implying that there is more than one covenant of grace, and this is affirmed by Mr Anthony Burgess[11] in his *Vindication of the Morall Law,* the 24th Lecture, text [Chapter] 4 of Deuteronomy.

5. Others with myself hold that there are but two Covenants, the one a Covenant of works, and the tree of life was a sacrament or sign and token of it; this was made with Adam before his fall and to all his posterity... But

9 Sidrach Simpson (c. 1600–1655) was a curate in London (1629–38) became an Independent in Rotterdam and returned to London as such in 1641.

10 Jeremiah Burroughs (c. 1599–1646) was assistant to Calamy 1627–31, then rector in Norfolk, then served in Rotterdam as an Independent from 1637 returning to London in 1641.

11 Anthony Burgess (1608–64) was a minister in Warwickshire and member of the Westminster Assembly, as also were Simpson and Burroughs. Stephen J. Casselli, *Divine Rule Maintained* (Grand Rapids: Reformation Heritage, 2016) examines the Covenant Theology of Burgess at length.

> then there was a Covenant of grace which God the Father made with Jesus Christ from all eternity to save some of the posterity of Adam…"[12]

Subsequent to this pamphlet the Westminster Assembly finalised its position on the Covenant. It recognised only two covenants, one of works, the other of grace (7.2–3), affirmed God's condescension in making the covenant of works (7.1), and of course rejected the intrinsic merit of our best works (16.5).

By stating that the *first* covenant with man was one of works with Adam (WCF 7.2), it rejected the position of those who denied a covenant of works with Adam (#3 above), but it left aside the question of a distinct covenant of redemption between the Father and the Son as advocated by some, such as Rutherford.

It also passed over that presentation of the covenant of grace combined with the so-called covenant of redemption held by Calamy (#5 above). In the Confession the second covenant noted (7.3)—the second with man (note the Chapter title, Of God's Covenant with Man)—provides for life and salvation by Jesus Christ and is one of grace, but the person or persons with whom it is made is either unspecified (WCF 7.3, WSC 20) or not well distinguished (WLC 31, 'Christ and the elect'), so giving room for views like Rutherford's and Calamy's. The intention is to allow liberty for those agreed on the substantial issue.

As for the Mosaic covenant, the Confession speaks of the covenant of grace being administered in the time of the law 'by promises, prophecies, sacrifices, circumcision, the paschal lamb, and other types and ordinances delivered to the people of the Jews' (7.5). It concludes: 'There are not therefore two covenants of

12 Edmund Calamy, *Two solemne Covenants*, 1–2.

grace differing in substance, but one and the same under different dispensations' (WCF 7.6), thus rejecting the view Calamy drew from Burgess (#4 above), and also closing the door to the notion of the covenant with Moses being a covenant of works in its essential nature (#2, 3 & 4). However, it does not exclude views of the Mosaic covenant that saw an aspect illustrative of the works-inheritance principle in it, subservient to its position as an administration of the covenant of grace. This was a quite common viewpoint.[13]

There is a certain tension in another aspect of the Westminster doctrine. Larger Catechism 93 seems to suggest a promise of life is attached to the moral law written on the heart, whereas WCF 7.1 suggests that reward could only come by way of God condescending to enter into covenant, of which the first with man was the covenant of works with Adam. WCF 19:1 appears to conflate the law on the heart and the arrangements in Genesis 2 under the term 'covenant' (cf. Savoy 19:1).

Savoy makes changes particularly in 6.1–3, but the Baptists omit explicit reference to the covenant of works with Adam in 7.2 and 19.1, retain it in 19.6, follow Savoy at 20.1 but not at 6.1. I doubt this is merely editorial.[14] Nevertheless, leading Particular Baptists used the expression and held the concept, but some in their circle may well have scrupled. On a related issue, Savoy (contra WCF) includes at 11.1 explicit reference to Christ's active obedience being imputed.[15]

---

13 Cf. Samuel Bolton, *True Bounds* (Edinburgh: Banner of Truth, 1994), 99.

14 Contra Samuel E. Waldron, *Exposition of the 1689 Confession* (Durham: Evangelical Press, 1989) 96, 479. The references retained are 19.1 (which does not tie to a pre-fall Adamic covenant) and 20.1 (which is, I suspect, an oversight by the compilers).

15 William Barker, *Puritan Profiles* (Fearn: Christian Focus, 1991), 158.

TABLE 3

WESTMINSTER CONFESSION, 1646	SAVOY DECLARATION, 1658	BAPTIST CONFESSION, 1677/1689
4.2: After God had made all other creatures, he created man, male and female, with reasonable and immortal souls, endued with knowledge, righteousness, and true holiness, after his own image; having the law of God written in their hearts, and power to fulfil it: and yet under a possibility of transgressing, being left to the liberty of their own will, which was subject unto change.	**4.2:** After God had made all other creatures, he created man, male and female, with reasonable and immortal souls, endued with knowledge, righteousness, and true holiness, after his own image; having the law of God written in their hearts, and power to fulfil it: and yet under a possibility of transgressing, being left to the liberty of their own will, which was subject unto change.	**4.2:** After God had made all other creatures, he created man, male and female, with reasonable and immortal souls, rendering them fit unto that life to God for which they were created; being made after the image of God, in knowledge, righteousness, and true holiness; having the law of God written in their hearts, and power to fulfil it, and yet under a possibility of transgressing, being left to the liberty of their own will, which was subject to change...
Besides the law written in their hearts, they received a command....	Besides the law written in their hearts, they received a command...	**4.3:** Besides the law written in their hearts, they received a command....
6.1: Our first parents, being seduced by the subtlety and temptation of Satan, sinned in eating the forbidden fruit. This their sin God was pleased, according to his wise and holy counsel, to permit, having purposed to order it to his own glory.	**6.1:** God having made a covenant of works and life, thereupon, with our first parents and all their posterity in them, they being seduced by the subtlety and temptation of Satan did wilfully transgress the law of their creation, and break the covenant in eating the forbidden fruit....	**6.1:** Although God created man upright and perfect, and gave him a righteous law, which had been unto life had he kept it, and threatened death upon the breach thereof, yet he did not long abide in this honour; Satan using the subtlety of the serpent to subdue Eve, then by her seducing Adam, who, without any compulsion, did wilfully transgress the law of their creation, and the command given unto them in eating the forbidden fruit, which God was pleased

		according to his wise and holy counsel to permit, having purposed to order it to his own glory.
6.2: By this sin they fell from their original righteousness...	**6.2:** By this sin they, and we in them, fell from original righteousness...	**6.2:** Our first parents, by this sin, fell from their original righteousness...
6.3: They being the root of all mankind, the guilt of this sin was imputed, and the same death in sin and corrupted nature conveyed, to all their posterity descending from them by ordinary generation.	**6.3**: They being the root, and by God's appointment, standing in the room and stead of all mankind, the guilt of this sin was imputed, and corrupted nature conveyed, to all their posterity descending from them by ordinary generation.	**6.3**: They being the root, and by God's appointment, standing in the room and stead of all mankind, the guilt of this sin was imputed, and corrupted nature conveyed, to all their posterity descending from them by ordinary generation, being now conceived in sin.
7.1: The distance between God and the creature is so great, that although reasonable creatures do owe obedience unto him as their Creator, yet they could never have any fruition of him as their blessedness and reward but by some voluntary condescension on God's part, which he hath been pleased to express by way of covenant.	**7.1**: The distance between God and the creature is so great, that although reasonable creatures do owe obedence unto him as their Creator, yet they could never have attained the reward of life but by some voluntary condescension on God's part, which he hath been pleased to express by way of covenant.	**7.1**: The distance between God and the creature is so great, that although reasonable creatures do owe obedience unto him as their Creator, yet they could never have attained the reward of life but by some voluntary condescension on God's part, which he hath been pleased to express by way of covenant.
7.2: The first covenant made with man was a covenant of works, wherein life was promised to Adam, and in him to his posterity, upon condition of perfect and personal obedience.	**7.2:** The first covenant made with man was a covenant of works, wherein life was promised to Adam, and in him to his posterity, upon condition of perfect and personal obedience.	

7.3: Man by his fall having made himself incapable of life by that covenant, the Lord was pleased to make a second, commonly called the covenant of grace...	**7.3**: Man by his fall having made himself incapable of life by that covenant, the Lord was pleased to make a second, commonly called the covenant of grace...	**7.2**: Moreover, man having brought himself under the curse of the law by his fall, it pleased the Lord to make a covenant of grace...
16.5: We cannot, by our best works, merit pardon of sin or eternal life at the hand of God, by reason of the great disproportion that is between them and the glory to come; and the infinite distance that is between us and God, of whom, by them, we can neither profit, nor satisfy for the debt of our former sins; but when we have done all we can, we have done but our duty, and are unprofitable servants...	**16.5**: We cannot, by our best works, merit pardon of sin or eternal life at the hand of God, by reason of the great disproportion that is between them and the glory to come; and the infinite distance that is between us and God, of whom, by them, we can neither profit, nor satisfy for the debt of our former sins; but when we have done all we can, we have done but our duty, and are unprofitable servants...	**16.5**: We cannot, by our best works, merit pardon of sin or eternal life at the hand of God, by reason of the great disproportion that is between them and the glory to come; and the infinite distance that is between us and God, of whom, by them, we can neither profit, nor satisfy for the debt of our former sins; but when we have done all we can, we have done but our duty, and are unprofitable servants...
19.1: God gave to Adam a law, as a covenant of works, by which he bound him and his posterity to personal, entire, exact and perpetual obedience; promised life upon the fulfilling, and threatened death upon the breach of it: and endued him with power and ability to keep it.	**19.1**: God gave to Adam a law of universal obedience written in his heart, and a particular precept of not eating the fruit of the tree of knowledge of good and evil, as a covenant of works, by which he bound him and his posterity to personal, entire, exact and perpetual obedience; promised life upon the fulfilling, and threatened death upon the breach of it: and endued him with power and ability to keep it.	**19.1**: God gave to Adam a law of universal obedience written in his heart, and a particular precept of not eating the fruit of the tree of knowledge of good and evil; by which he bound him and his posterity to personal, entire, exact and perpetual obedience; promised life upon the fulfilling, and threatened death upon the breach of it: and endued him with power and ability to keep it.
19.6: Although true believers be not under the law as a covenant of works, to be thereby justified or condemned....	**19.6**: Although true believers be not under the law as a covenant of works, to be thereby justified or condemned....	**19.6**: Although true believers be not under the law as a covenant of works, to be thereby justified or condemned....

(no parallel)	**20.1**: The covenant of works being broken by sin, and made unprofitable unto life, God was pleased to give forth the promise of Christ...	**20.1**: The covenant of works being broken by sin, and made unprofitable unto life, God was pleased to give forth the promise of Christ...

It is worth noting that the proof text supporting the existence of the covenant of works with Adam in WCF 7.2 is Galatians 3:12.[16] Although this text on the surface might seem to be applicable only to a principle of works-inheritance associated with the Sinai covenant, the tradition of interpretation had seen this principle operative prior to Sinai. The citation needs to be considered in that light. The Savoy did not append Scripture texts.

In the next chapter note is taken of Rutherford, Sedgwick, Bridge and Strong, who were also members of the Westminster Assembly but who wrote on the covenant after the Assembly's doctrinal work was completed.

16 Westminster would have preferred to omit the illustrative texts and included them only at the insistence of Parliament.

6

COCCEIUS AND LATER, 1648–1700

Johannes Cocceius (1603–1669) is important. Cocceius was born into a well-connected family in Bremen. Much of his study was done at Franeker where William Ames was one of his teachers. He taught successively at Bremen, Franeker and Leiden. Over against the tendency to use systematic theology as an interpretative grid, Cocceius aimed to draw his theology from careful contextual exposition of Scripture in the light of the unfolding purpose of God in Christ. He was thus in many ways the founder of biblical theology. Most of his works are biblical exposition. His *Summa Doctrinae de Foedere et Testamento* was published at Leiden in 1648, and was a presentation of biblical teaching structured by the covenant idea. He rejected the Scholastic emphasis on the absolute will of God which did not give proper weight to the character of God by which his will is regulated. Cocceius' covenant thought in balanced form is represented well by Witsius.

In the 1660s a protracted dispute broke out between dogmaticians such as Gisbertus Voetius of Utrecht and Cocceius and his followers, in which there was much over-reaction on all sides and no truly fundamental differences when all was boiled down. Some of Cocceius' exegesis was fanciful, and he pressed the distinction between law and gospel more strongly than was usual, taking a more liberal view of the Sabbath in the process.

Thomas Blake (c. 1597–1657) graduated MA from Oxford. He published his *Vindiciæ Foederis, or, A Treatise of the Covenant of God entered with man-kinde in the several kindes and degrees of it....* in 1653. A second enlarged edition was issued after his death with two sermons given at his funeral, one by Anthony Burgess.

David Dickson (c. 1583–1663) is of importance as an early advocate of the covenant of redemption between the Father and the Son, and for his joint authorship with **James Durham** (1622–58) of *The Sum of Saving Knowledge* published in 1650. It is traditionally bound with the Subordinate Standards of the Church of Scotland although it has never had Assembly sanction.

TABLE 4

THE SUM OF SAVING KNOWLEDGE, 1650

Head 1: Our woeful condition by nature, through breaking the covenant of works.

Hosea 13.9 "O Israel, thou hast destroyed thyself."

I. The almighty and eternal God, the Father, the Son, and the Holy Ghost, three distinct persons in the one and the same undivided Godhead, equally infinite in all perfections, did, before time, most wisely decree, for his own glory, whatsoever cometh to pass in time: and doth most holily and infallibly execute all his decrees, without being partaker of the sin of any creature.

II. This God, in six days, made all things of nothing, very good in their own kind: in special, he made all the angels holy; and he made our first parents, Adam and Eve, the root of mankind, both upright and able to keep the law written in their heart. Which law they were naturally bound to obey under pain of death; but God was not bound to reward their service, till he entered into a covenant or contract with them, and their posterity in them, to give them eternal life, upon condition of perfect personal obedience; withal threatening death in case they should fail. This is the covenant of works.

III. Both angels and men were subject to the change of their own free will, as experience proved, (God having reserved to himself the incommunicable property of being naturally unchangable:) for many angels of their own accord fell by sin from their first estate and became devils. Our first parents, being enticed by Satan, one of these devils speaking in a serpent, did break the covenant of works, in eating the forbidden fruit; whereby they, and their posterity, being in their loins, as branches in the root, and comprehended in the same covenant with them, became not only liable to eternal death, but also lost all ability to please God; yea, did become by nature enemies to God, and to all spiritual good, and inclined only to evil continually. This is our original sin, the bitter root of all our actual transgressions, in thought, word, and deed.

Samuel Rutherford (c. 1600–61), a complex man,[1] was one of the Scottish Commissioners to the Westminster Assembly and a scholar with an international reputation. His *Covenant of Life Opened* (Edinburgh 1655) is his most specific work on the covenants of works and grace, but is surpassed in clarity and comprehensiveness by **Patrick Gillespie** (1617–75), brother of George and Principal of Glasgow University. His *The Ark of the Covenant Opened* was issued in two parts. The first volume (in 1661) covers the covenants of works and grace in some 550 pages; the second instalment (1677) has nearly 500 pages on the covenant of redemption and the mediatorial work of Christ. Volumes on the instrumentality of faith, and the privileges and duties of the covenant were projected but never published. The great John Owen commended the second volume highly: 'I do freely declare my judgment, that for order, method, perspicuity in treating, and solidity of argument, the ensuing discourse exceeds whatsover single treatise I have seen written with the same design.'[2]

1 The definitive biography is John Coffey, *Politics, Religion and the British Revolutions: The Mind of Samuel Rutherford* (Cambridge 1997).

2 Cf. James Walker, *The Theology and Theologians of Scotland 1560–1750*, 20.

Another Westminster divine who wrote on the covenants was **Obadiah Sedgwick** (c. 1600–58), a Presbyterian and the father-in-law of Thomas Manton. After studies at Oxford he was for a period a chaplain in the Netherlands. He was noted as a lively and popular preacher. He prepared *The Bowels of Tender Mercy in the Everlasting Covenant* before he died and his friends saw it through the press in 1661.

William Bridge (c. 1600–71) was educated at Cambridge, deprived of his Norwich parish in 1637 for non-conformity, and settled in Rotterdam as an Independent pastor for some years before returning to England. He was a member of the Westminster Assembly. Ten of his sermons 'lately taken by an expert hearer' were published as *Christ and the Covenant* in 1667.

Yorkshire-born **Francis Roberts** (1608–75) graduated MA from Trinity College, Oxford in 1632 and joined the Presbyterian party at the beginning of the Civil War. He was pastor of the church at Wrington in Somerset from 1649 until his death. He wrote a number of books. *His Mysterium & Medulla Bibliorum: The Mystery and Marrow of the Bible, viz: God's Covenant...* was the fruit of his weekly lectures from September 1651 to May 1657, and extends to some 1700 pages of well organised material totalling more than 750,000 words![3] It does not seem obvious to me that Roberts was familiar with Cocceius, but he made good use of earlier English writers and Europeans such as Calvin, the great Lutheran dogmatician, Johann Gerhard (1582–1637) of Jena, and the celebrated Reformed teachers, J.H. Alsted (1588–1638) and André Rivet (1572–1651). The latter was influential in drawing up

3 *The Covenant Theology of Francis Roberts* by Won Taek Lim is a PhD thesis which was completed under the supervision of members of the faculty of Calvin Theological Seminary, Grand Rapids in 2000.

the important *Synopsis purioris theologicæ* (Leiden, 1625) which defended Reformed doctrine.

John Barret (1631–1713) graduated MA from Emmanuel College, Cambridge and became Presbyterian minister in Nottingham in 1656. He was ejected in 1662 but continued to hold conventicles. In 1675 he published *Good will towards men, or A Treatise of the Covenants viz: Of works, and of grace: old and new...* This is clearly written, with pages 1–105 discussing the covenant of works in terms of distinct propositions.

In 1675 the *Helvetic Consensus Formula*, drafted by **J.H. Heidegger** (1633–98) to deal with the theology of Saumur, was agreed by the Synod of Zurich and was specific on the covenant of works. (Table 5) It was strongly supported by Francis Turretin at Geneva where it was adopted in 1678. For various unrelated reasons this Formula did not achieve generally accepted status, and even in Switzerland did not long endure. Nevertheless, it is a witness to the view of the covenant of works at that time.

The *Second London Confession* of the English Particular, or Calvinistic, Baptists was published in 1677 as a revision of the Savoy, and reaffirmed in 1689. The relevant sections have been set out in Table 3 in the previous chapter.

Herman Witsius (1636–1708) was born not far from Amsterdam the son of the local magistrate, and received an excellent education at Groningen, Leiden and Utrecht. In 1675, after some years in pastoral work, he was appointed Professor of theology at Franeker, five years later moving to a similar post at Utrecht, and in 1697 moving to Leiden. In 1677 he published the book by which he is perhaps best known, *De Œconomia foederum*

Dei cum homnibus. The 2nd edition was issued in 1685, a third in 1694, and further printings in 1714 and 1739. It was translated into English and published in London in 1763 as *The Economy of the Covenants Between God and Man.* It had at least seven printings in the United Kingdom: 1763 (London), 1774 (Dublin), 1775 (London), 1803 (Edinburgh), 1804, 1822, 1837, and two in America: 1798/99 (New York), 1804. A Dutch translation was issued in 1716. Witsius' aim was to conciliate the factionalism which had arisen between the systematicians, such as the followers of Voetius, and the followers of Cocceius. His presentation of Covenant Theology is often winsomely and movingly expressed.

William Strong (d. 1654) was educated at Cambridge and became a Fellow of St Catherine's Hall in 1631. He was later preacher at Westminster Abbey and was appointed to the Westminster Assembly in 1645. He signed a recommendation of the second edition of *The Marrow of Moderne Divinitie.* Most of his work was published soon after his death but one item was not published until 1678, his *A Discourse on the Two Covenants.*

Francis Turretin (1623–87) was the son of a Reformed pastor-theologian at Geneva although the family origins were in Italy, hence the original of his name (Turretini). Francis became pastor of the Italian congregation in Geneva 1648–51, and then pastored the church at Leiden 1651–52 when Cocceius was there. In 1653 he was appointed Professor of theology at Geneva. He was a careful theologian. His great Latin work, now happily published in English, was entitled *Institutes of Elenctic Theology* (3 vols. 1679/85). This title indicates a polemical (elenctic) theology is presented, so he concentrates on issues of current debate rather than providing a

TABLE 5

HELVETIC CONSENSUS, 1675

Canon 7: As all his works were known to God from eternity [Acts 15:18], so in time, according to his infinite power, wisdom, and goodness, he made man, the glory and end of his works, in his own image, and, therefore, upright, wise, and just. Having created man in this manner, he put him under the covenant of works, and in this covenant freely promised him communion with God, favour and life, if indeed he acted in obedience to his will.

Canon 8: Moreover that promise connected to the covenant of works was not a continuation only of earthly life and happiness but the possession especially of eternal and celestial life, a life namely, of both body and soul in heaven, if indeed man ran the course of perfect obedience, with unspeakable joy in communion with God. For not only did the Tree of Life prefigure this very thing unto Adam, but the power of the law, which, being fulfilled by Christ, who went under it in our place, awards to us nothing other than celestial life in Christ who kept the same righteousness of the law. The power of the law also threatens man with both temporal and eternal death.

Canon 9: Wherefore we can not agree with the opinion of those who deny that a reward of heavenly bliss was offered to Adam on condition of obedience to God. We also do not admit that the promise of the covenant of works was nothing more than a promise of perpetual life abounding in every kind of good that can be suited to the body and soul of man in a state of perfect nature, and the enjoyment thereof in an earthly Paradise. For this also is contrary to the sound sense of the Divine Word, and weakens the power of the law considered in itself.

Canon 10: God entered into the covenant of works not only with Adam for himself, but also, in him as the head and root with the whole human race. Man would, by virtue of the blessing of the nature derived from Adam, inherit also the same perfection, provided he continued in it. So Adam by his sorrowful fall sinned and lost the benefits promised in the covenant not only for himself, but also for the whole human race that would be born by the flesh. We hold, therefore, that the sin of Adam is imputed by the mysterious and just judgment of God to all his posterity. For the Apostle testifies that "in Adam all sinned, by one man's disobedience many were made sinners" [Rom 5:12,19] and "in Adam all die" [I Cor 15:21–22]. But there appears no way in which hereditary corruption could fall, as a spiritual death, upon the whole human race by the just judgment of God, unless some sin of that race preceded, incurring the penalty of that death. For God, the most supreme Judge of all the earth, punishes none but the guilty.

Canon 11: For a double reason, therefore, man, because of sin, is by nature, and hence from his birth, before committing any actual sin, exposed to God's wrath and curse; first, on account of the transgression and disobedience which he committed in the loins of Adam; and, secondly, on account of the consequent hereditary corruption implanted to his very conception, whereby his whole nature is depraved and spiritually dead; so that original sin may rightly be regarded as twofold, imputed sin and inherent hereditary sin.

Canon 12: Accordingly we can not, without harm to the Divine truth, agree with those who deny that Adam represented his posterity by God's intention, and that his sin is imputed, therefore, immediately to his posterity; and under this mediate and consequent imputation not only destroy the imputation of the first sin, but also expose the doctrine of hereditary corruption to grave danger.

Translated by Martin I. Klauber, *Trinity Journal* 11 (1990): 103–23, and slightly amended by the present writer.

full systematic theology.[4] It's pretty full nonetheless! This theology was widely used in Scotland in the 18th century, and formed the basis of Charles Hodge's teaching at Princeton Theological Seminary in the 19th century.

On a more popular level, the justly esteemed **John Bunyan** (1628–88), an open communion Baptist, published *The Doctrine of the Law and Grace Unfolded* in 1685 in which he likewise taught the covenant of works with Adam.

In 1681 **Nehemiah Coxe** (d. 1689), the English Baptist, who at one time served with Bunyan, published *A Discourse of the Covenants that God made with Men before the Law Wherein the Covenant of Circumcision is more largely handled and the Invalidity of the Plea for Paedobaptism taken from thence discovered* (London: printed by J.D.). Coxe was a closed communion Particular Baptist who had input into the 1677 Baptist Confession. He is quite clear on the covenant of works with Adam. His distinctive viewpoint, building on John Tombes, is to regard the covenants with Abraham and Moses as essentially legal covenants which require obedience to gain the blessing. So, he held, they are not actual administrations of the one covenant of grace, as was the general Reformed position, although there is a sense, he said, in which they point forward to the covenant of grace. That covenant in its true unconditional character arises only when Christ fulfils the covenant of works on behalf of his people so enabling the bestowal of a free and unconditional salvation on the elect.

4 Cf. Francis Turretin, *Institutes of Elenctic Theology* (Phillipsburg: P & R, 1992), I. 4.

In 1693 the Classis Walcheren in the province of Zeeland, the Netherlands, adopted five articles on points that had been disputed. They had in view the liberal-rationalist teachings of Balthasar Bekker, H. A. Roëll and Johannes Vlak who also rejected the covenant of works as a doctrine only 60 or 70 years old. Article 4 [Of the Imputation of Adam's Sin] is relevant to the covenant of works, which is referred to near the end.[5]

5 As far as I am aware no other discussion of the Walcheren Articles is available in English, but see the relevant entries in F.W.Grosheide & G.P.Van Itterzon (eds.), *Christelijke Encylopaedie* (Kampen: Kok, 1961).

TABLE 6

Art. 4, WALCHEREN ARTICLES, 1693

'The position of the first man in paradise and the Command of Life given to him [Belgic Confession Art.14], was that he there took the place of the whole human race. So that the image of God and all the gifts which he himself received from god and lost by his sin, he received and lost not only for himself, but also for all his descendants. [Heidelberg Catechism question 9]

Consequently Adam's sin regards us too, because all men had been in that one man as children in the loins of the father of all [Summary Heid. Cat. question 11], and as co-members in the Head and Principal of their covenant, this is how we all have sinned in him.

We are of the conviction that among the bad implications of this sin, which fall upon all Adam's children, are the deprival of God's image and congenital corruption [Heid.Cat.q.7 and 9], being spiritual death and consequently part of the threat: In the day that thou eatest thereof, thou shalt surely die. [Genesis 2:17]. This then is considered by us not only to be an evil of sin but also as an evil of punishment, lying on all people, and having no other foundation than Adam's transgression.

Furthermore, because we have not committed this sin, so can the guilt of it not become ours except by way of Imputation [Romans 5:13), which imputation is not to be understood as to be metaphorical and made by means of our intervening corruption, but in this way that the guilt of Adam's disobedience is transferred and made common to all men in a real and direct way, so that we all are guilty of (and deserve) the curse and eternal death; [Canons of Dort I,1; Romans 5:18] and by the transgression of one person the guilt has come upon all men unto damnation.

Therefore we acknowledge God in His wise prudence concerning the state and fall of the first man, not only as an almighty Creator, but also as a righteous Judge (For all His ways are judgment) [Deuteronomy 32:4; Heid. Cat.q 4; Canons of Dort III/IV, 2], Who according to His righteous judgment finds the guilt of His offended majesty in this first transgression and punished it in all men with temporal and eternal punishments.

Over against this we also, to our comfort, learn from Paul that in this respect Adam was a figure of Him that was to come [Romans 5:14)]. So that these two are opposites, Adam as the Head of all who were in the covenant of works, (and) Christ as the Head of all who are in the covenant of grace. And as by one man's disobedience many were made sinners, so by the obedience of one shall many be made righteous, [Romans 5:19] in such a way that, as Adam's disobedience is imputed to us as a guilt that deserves damnation, so Christ's obedience is imputed to us as releasing us from this guilt.

Therefore (together with the Synod of Charenton, held in 1644) we condemn the opinion that original sin was determined only by the congenital corruption, with the exclusion of the imputation of Adam's guilt, as being in conflict with the opinion of all Protestant Churches.

Translation through the kindness of Rev Gerald van Rongen, Kelmscott, Western Australia. Subscription to these articles was in force in Classis Walcheren until 1816.

7

REVIEW

Various factors have been suggested to explain the sudden appearance of the covenant of works. These include trade, social and political influences as well as the impact of Ramist logic in its use of dichotomy to bring out the nature of things. Some early covenant theologians such as Polanus, Rollock and Ames were strongly influenced by Ramus. But it was also natural for theological refinement to occur as Protestantism moved from existence as a Protest movement 'to its destiny as a self-sufficient ecclesiastical establishment with its own distinct academic, confessional and dogmatic needs.'[1] However, the move is really from implicit to explicit.

The covenant of works with Adam is not as such a revolutionary departure from the views of early Reformers such as Calvin, since Christ's work as the Last Adam is clearly a covenantal work.[2] Jesus himself refers to 'the new covenant in my blood', and passages such as Romans 5:12ff, and 1 Corinthians 15:22 draw parallels between

1 Richard A. Muller, *God, Creation and Providence in the Thought of Jacob Arminius* (Grand Rapids: Baker, 1991), 4–5.

2 P.A.Lillback, *The Binding of God* (Grand Rapids: Baker, 2001) 276–304 discusses the question 'Is there a Covenant of Works in Calvin's Theology?' and illustrates the point made.

Adam and Christ.[3] The 19th century covenant theologian Hugh Martin states:

> "...it is more from what is partly the analogy and partly the antithesis of the two covenants, when set forth in the mutual light which they reflect on each other, that the covenant of works becomes manifest, than in any very express or abundant evidence of its own alone."[4]

Paul uses the story of Sarah and Hagar to represent two covenants (Gal. 4:21ff). This is significant since they lived before Moses.[5] To see the covenants they symbolise as quite opposite, as Paul does, suggests a covenant of law and bondage existed in Abrahams' time as well as a covenant of grace and freedom. Given that the covenant at Sinai did not annul the promise to Abraham (Gal. 3:17), and was not in itself a covenant of works, even if some were in effect using it that way, there must have been a legal covenant before Moses, namely a covenant with Adam who had the law written on his heart but broke it. Some such was one of a number of likely chains of reasoning.[6] It was certainly an easy and logical step to recognise the First Adam as standing in a covenantal relationship with God. The covenant requiring obedience, which was broken by Adam, was seen as fulfilled by Jesus Christ in accordance with covenant made with Abraham.

---

3 As far as I can see, 1 Corinthians 15:42–49 was rarely cited in the literature, apparently not being seen as having relevance to the eschatology of the pre-fall state of humanity; exceptions include William Bucanus and Samuel Rutherford.

4 *The Atonement in its relations to the Covenant, the Priesthood, the Intercession of our Lord* (Edinburgh: Knox Press, 1976), 35.

5 Rollock uses the analogy of Sarah and Hagar in Chapter 2 of his *Treatise on Effectual Calling* (1597) when dealing with the covenant of works.

6 In 1661, Patrick Gillespie, apparently not aware of the origin in the late 1580s, offers a proof of the covenant of works by reasoning back from Galatians 4:24 in the terms summarised in this paragraph (*Ark of the Covenant*, 181–183).

Jesus, Abraham's offspring, obtained salvation for his people by his perfect obedience to the Father.

PART THREE

THE EXPOSITION OF THE COVENANT OF WORKS TO 1700

We have seen that prior to Polanus a pre-fall covenant with Adam was sometimes referred to but only in the sense of a binding law or unconditional promise, and this was grounded in his creation in God's image. The term covenant of nature or covenant of creation was usual for this. Polanus begins a tradition of identifying the arrangement in Genesis 2:16–17 as a post-creation covenant, most usually called the covenant of works.

We commonly use the term covenant to refer to mutual agreements and contracts. However, it may also refer to dispositions by a superior party to an inferior, as by ancient rulers to their vassals. In Greek the word for the mutually negotiated contract is suntheke, and for the unilateral disposition it is diatheke. The latter term is the one used in Scripture for God's covenants.

Reformed theologians were always conscious of God's initiative in making covenants with humanity, always conscious that he was Creator and we dependent creatures. So God's covenants with humanity were seen as commitments from him normally requiring the discharge of obligations by us. Their origin and terms were from God, but their administration involved both parties since they committed to mutual faithfulness in the covenant relation. However, God's covenant is not a business contract implying possible mistrust, but a bond in love between friends.

John Barret (1675) rightly reminds us: 'Men that Covenant one with another, aim each at their own advantage; but God in Covenanting with his Creatures, does not expect any benefit or advantage by them, but does it to show how willing and ready he is to communicate his benefits to them.'[1]

1 John Barret, *Good Will Towards Men*, 44.

8

COVENANT DEFINED

The term covenant is recognised as used in a variety of ways in Scripture. When used in theology of the arrangement with pre-fall Adam the mutual aspect is usually stressed, and the use of a sign or token confirming the covenant is usually noted (for which see Chapter 16 below).

Polanus (1589): 'God's covenant is a bargain which God has made with men, in which God promises to men some good, and requires of them again, that they perform those things which he commands. And that covenant is either eternal or temporal. The eternal covenant is a covenant in which God promises men eternal life. And that is two-fold, the covenant of works, or the covenant of grace. The covenant of works is a bargain of God made with men concerning eternal life, to which is both a condition of perfect obedience adjoined, to be performed by man, and also a threatening of eternal death if he shall not perform perfect obedience. Genesis 2:17.'[1]

Rollock (1597): 'The covenant of God generally is a promise under some one certain condition.'[2]

---

1 A Polanus, *The Substance of Christian Religion Soundly Set Forth in two books by definitions and partitions framed according to the rules of a natural method* [translated from the Latin by Elijah Wilcocks] (London: John Oxenbridge, 1595) 87–88.

2 Robert Rollock, *A Treatise of God's Effectual Calling*, 6.

Ames (1623): '...the law of God or his covenant with man in the creation was, Do this and you will live; if you do it not you shall die.'[3]

Ussher compilation (1625/45): 'What understand you by a Covenant? An agreement which it pleases Almighty God to enter into with man concerning his everlasting condition.'[4]

Leigh (1633): 'A Covenant is a solemn Contract, passing between some parties (two at the least) whereby they bind themselves, each to the other in certain articles to both their contents, for their mutual peace and comfort. For the form and manner of it, it must be done with some solemnity; and herein stands the difference between a promise and a Covenant, for a Covenant is a bundle of promises, bound and knit up together in one tie and mutual solemnity.'[5]

Ball (d. 1640) 'The [term] Covenant in Scripture doth sometimes signify an absolute promise of God, without any stipulation at all, such as was the covenant God made with Noah... But sometimes in holy Writ the name Covenant is so used that it plainly signified a free Promise of God, but with stipulation of duty from the reasonable creature...For a covenant is a *quiddam complexum* [a complex thing], implying two things distinguished either *re* or *ratione*, the one covenanting and the other restipulating or accepting. As also two parts covenanted. First the giving of some future good. Secondly the retribution of some performance. For the first without the second is no more than a Promise and the second without the first no less than a Law...The Covenant

3 William Ames, *Medulla Theologica* (1623) translated by J.D.Eusden as *The Marrow of Theology* (Durham NC: Labyrinth, 1983) I.X.32 (p.113).
4 James Ussher, *A Body of Divinity* (London 1645), 123.
5 Edward Leigh, *A Treatise of the Divine Promises* (London, 1633), 63.

which God made with our first parents is that mutual contract or agreement, wherein God promised eternal happiness to man upon condition of entire and perfect obedience to be performed in his own person.'[6]

Burgess (1647): (unlike a law or a testament) '...a Covenant doth require consent and agreement between two parties.[7]

Blake (1658): 'The essentials or real properties of a covenant... are in short comprised in these words, A mutual consent of parties with stipulations both sides.'[8]

Roberts (1657): 'The Covenant which God made with the first Adam and his posterity before the fall...is God's gracious Agreement with Adam, and with his Posterity, in him, to give them eternal life and happiness upon condition of perfect and personal obedience.'[9]

Bridge (1667): '[A covenant] is a *mutual agreement*, and herein a Covenant differs from a Law. A Law properly is a commandment with penalty. No sooner was man made, but he was under a Law, to be obedient unto God his Maker; and in case he broke it, God by the Law of Nature might punish him. But then when God said unto him, In the day that thou eatest thereof, thou shalt die the death, then God entered into a Covenant, man accepting thereof.'[10]

---

6 John Ball, *A Treatise of the Covenant of Grace*, (London: E. Brewster, 1645) 3–4, 9. There is much that is verbally identical with Ball's definition in John Cameron's 1608 presentation, cf. B.G.Armstrong, *Calvin and the Amyraut Heresy* (Wisconsin: Wisconsin University Press, 1969), 47ff.

7 Anthony Burgess, *Vindiciae Legis, or A Vindication of the Morall Law and the Covenants* (London: Thomas Underhill, 2nd ed. 1647), 124.

8 Thomas Blake, *Vindiciae Foederis,* 2nd ed., 1648, 11.

9 Francis Roberts, *Mysterium*, 24.

10 William Bridge, *Christ and the Covenant*, 58, who quotes the Geneva Bible.

Witsius (1677): 'A covenant of God with man is an agreement between God and man about the way of obtaining consummate happiness; including a threat of eternal destruction with which the one contemptuous of the happiness offered in that way is to be punished.'[11]

---

11 Herman Witsius, *Oeconomia Foederum Dei cum homnibus* (1677) 3rd ed 1694 translated by William Cruikshank as *The Economy of the Covenants between God and Man* [1763] (London 1822) I.i.ix (p.45), language slightly modernised

9

IS THERE A COVENANT WITH ADAM?

It is not until the 20th century that real attention is given to Genesis 1 as significant in understanding a covenant relation with Adam. In the early writers the focus is on the arrangement in Genesis 2. The understanding of the covenant relation is both inferred from later Scriptures and brought to Genesis 2, and inferred from Genesis 2 without drawing on the positive material in Genesis 1 to any great extent.

In Rollock's work (1597) there is no reference to the absence of the actual term in Genesis 1–3, and the same is true of Ball (1615) and Ames (1623). The fact of a covenant relationship is simply assumed from the text—a revealing fact itself. As already noted (page 60), **Bucanus** (d. 1603) does not use the term 'covenant' although he draws the same conclusions as those who did. Later, **John Ball** (d. 1640), in his major work posthumously published during the Westminster Assembly, offers a justification: 'We read not the word Covenant between God and man, ever since the Creation, both in Innocency, and under the fall; but we have in Scripture what may amount to as much. As in Innocency God provided and proposed to Adam, eternal happiness in the present enjoyments, and calls for perfect obedience: which appears from God's threatening, Genesis

2:17. For if man must die if he disobeyed, it implies strongly that God's covenant was with him for life, if he obeyed.'[1] Or again, 'We read not in Scripture, the covenant of works, or of grace *totidem syllabis* [= in as many words]. The nearest we come to it is Romans 3:27, the Law of works opposed to the Law of faith; which holds out as much as the Covenant of works and the Covenant of Grace.'[2]

In 1657 **Francis Roberts** offers four points: (1) God's writing his law on Adam's heart was itself an implicit covenant of works; (2) the positive law given verbally to Adam illustrates parties covenanting; (3) the intended use of the two trees in the garden was sacramental of the covenant terms, assuring of life for obedience and death for disobedience; (4) according to Romans 5:12f in Adam's sin we all sinned, and as his sin is not actually ours it must be ours by imputation, which is founded on Adam's position as a representative or public person in covenant for himself and his posterity.[3]

This agrees for substance with the presentation offered by **William Strong** (d. 1654), a member of the Westminster Assembly, in his posthumously published work on the covenants, and by **Anthony Burgess,** another noted member of the same Assembly. Burgess states: 'We are not therefore to be so rigid, as to call for express places, which do name this Covenant; for that which is necessarily and immediately drawn from Scripture, is as truly Scripture, as that which is expressly contained in it.'[4]

1 John Ball, *A Treatise of the Covenant of Grace*, 6. This passage is reproduced verbatim in Edward Fisher, *The Marrow of Modern Divinity*, 2nd and subsequent editions.

2 John Ball, *A Treatise of the Covenant of Grace*, 9.

3 Francis Roberts, Mysterium, 20–22.

4 William Strong, *A Discourse of the Two Covenants…* (London: F. Tyton & T. Parkhurst, 1678) 2; Anthony Burgess, *Vindiciæ Legis, or, A Vindication of the Morall Law and the Covenants* (London: Thomas Underhill, 1647), 122–124.

The master English theologian **John Owen** (1616–83) notes in the first of his volumes on Hebrews published in 1668: 'That God created man in and under the terms and law of a covenant, with a prescription of duties and promise of reward, is by all acknowledged.'[5]

Turretin (1679) establishes the existence of a covenant with Adam thus: (1) there are contracting parties, God and man; (2) there is a law imposed, and the threat for disobedience implies the promise of life as was also pledged by the tree of life; (3) Hosea 6:7 seems to refer to Adam breaking covenant; (4) the goodness of God demands that the man should be brought to fulfilment by means of a covenant of blessing.[6]

---

5 John Owen, *An Exposition of the Epistle to the Hebrews* [ed. W.H.Goold, 1855] (Grand Rapids: Baker, 1990) Vol 1., 78.

6 Francis Turretin, *Institutes*, I. 576–577.

10

NAMING THE COVENANT WITH ADAM

The names given to the pre-fall covenant vary since one can look at the relationship of God and Adam from different angles. As the original relationship, to be fulfilled through use of the endowments given him, it may be called the covenant of *creation* or of *nature*. Being made with Adam before sin it may be called the covenant of *innocence*. As made between parties who were friends it may be called the covenant of *friendship* or of *love* [but not of *reconciliation*, which implies disagreement when there was none]. The blessing in view may lead us to call it a covenant of *life*, (although it was also a covenant of *death* if disobeyed), while the requirement of obedience to God suggests the term *legal* covenant or covenant of *law* or of *works* or of *obedience*. Consideration of the tender love and generosity God showed may suggest the term covenant of *favour*.

Rollock (1597): 'The covenant of works, which may also be called a legal or natural covenant, is founded in nature, which was pure and holy, and in the law of God, which was in the first creation engraved in man's heart. For after God had created man after his own image, pure and holy, and had written his law in his mind, he made a covenant with man. In it he promised him eternal life upon the condition of good and holy works which should correspond to the holiness and goodness of their creation and conform to his law.'[1]

In 1608, **John Cameron** (c. 1579–1625) presented his triple covenant view at Heidelberg. He distinguished the covenant of nature, the covenant of *grace* and the *foedus gratiae subserviens* (or, *foedus vetus,* old covenant) meaning by the last the temporary Mosaic dispensation.[2] In 1633, **Edward Leigh** (1602–71) distinguished a legal and an evangelical covenant, although in his discussion he also calls the former a covenant of nature and a covenant of works.[3] **Ball** (d. 1640) does not seem concerned about nomenclature: 'Some distinguish thus, the Covenant is either of Nature or of Grace, or subservient to both which is called the Old Testament. Others thus, the Covenant is Legal or Evangelical, of works or of grace...'[4]

Samuel Bolton (1645) was one who preferred to speak of three covenants, of works, of grace, and a third (the Mosaic) subservient to the covenant of grace and including temporal promises to Israel. However, he admits the more general opinion was for two covenants only, of works and of grace.[5]

William Strong (d. 1654) speaks in this way: 'The Covenant God made is double according to the twofold state of Man. (1) In his state of Integrity. And this was *foedus amicitiae*, a Covenant of

1 Robert Rollock, *A Treatise of God's Effectual Calling*, 6–7 (I have slightly modernised the translator's language).

2 Thesis 7 in the 1608 work; cf. B.G.Armstrong, *Calvin and the Amyraut Heresy*, 52ff.

3 Edward Leigh, *A Treatise of the Divine Promises* (London, 1633) facing page 1, 63.

4 John Ball, *A Treatise of the Covenant of Grace,* 8.

5 Samuel Bolton, *The True Bounds*.(Edinburgh reprint 1974),

friendship between persons never at variance: (2) In his state of Corruption. When man by sin had broken the first, and brought himself under the curse thereof, then God brought in the Covenant of reconciliation, and that was *foedus misericordiae*, that is, a Covenant of Mercy.'[6]

In the productions of the Assembly of Divines at Westminster covenant of works is used in the Confession 7:2, and covenant of *life* in Larger Catechism 20 and Shorter Catechism 12. Clearly there was no great concern about the precise language used if the thing itself was granted.

Thomas Blake (d. 1657) writes: The former [covenant] is usually called a covenant of Works, the latter is called a covenant of Grace, though, indeed, the fountain and first rise of either was the free grace and favour of God.'[7]

Francis Roberts (1657) prefers to distinguish the two covenants as that of works in the first Adam before the fall, and of faith in the second Adam after the fall, citing Romans 3:27; 4:13 as illustrative of the appropriateness of such a distinction. Under the covenant of faith he thinks of six covenants of promise (with Adam, Noah, Abraham, Israel at Sinai, David, the exiled Jews) climaxed by the new covenant or covenant of performance. Citing Polanus, Roberts is not happy with his terminology of works and of grace for the two covenants since, he says, there is also divine favour in the first. He also dislikes Leigh's nomenclature since 'legal' can confuse the Mosaic covenant with the pre-fall covenant, but if this meaning is avoided then the terms are the same for substance with works

---

6 William Strong, *A Discourse*, 2.
7 William Blake, *Vindiciae Foederis* (London, 1658), 9.

and faith, he claims. Nor does he think Cameron's terminology suitable.[8]

Sedgwick (d. 1658): 'Foedus Nature (as some style it) or Foedus operum, the Covenant of works as we usually call it; the Apostle calls it the Law of works (Rom. 3:27). This is the Covenant which God made with man in the state of innocency before the fall...'[9]

Patrick Gillespie rejects Cameron's third covenant, holding that if it existed distinct from the covenants of law and grace, it would either offer 'righteousness and life upon some other terms than Works or Faith; or else it should be a covenant of mixed nature, that stood partly of Works, and partly of Grace', but neither of these is possible according to Scripture (e.g. Rom. 10:5–6; 4:4–6; 11:6).[10]

Turretin (1679) comments: 'It [the Adamic covenant] is called "natural" not from natural obligation (which God does not have toward man), but because it is founded on the nature of man (as it was at first created by God) and on his integrity and powers. It is also called "legal" because the condition on man's part was the observation of the law of nature engraved within him; and of "works" because it depended on works or his proper obedience.'[11]

Nehemiah Coxe (1681) 'This covenant that God made with Adam, and all mankind in him, as to the Terms and Conditions of it (we see) was a Covenant of Works; with respect to the immediate privilege and relation, it was a Covenant of Friendship, and with regard to the reward promised, it was a Covenant of rich Bounty

8 Francis Roberts, *Mysterium*, 16–19.
9 Obadiah Sedgwick, *The Bowels of Tender Mercy*, 6.
10 Patrick Gillespie, *The Ark* (1661), 153–157.
11 Francis Turretin, *Institutes*, I, 575.

and Goodness, but included not, nor intimated the least iota of pardoning mercy...'[12]

12 Nehemiah Coxe, *A Discourse of the Covenants*, 29.

11

LAW AND COVENANT: THE TWO STATES OF THE PRE-FALL ADAM

The transaction in Genesis 2:16–17 involves a specific prohibition in a matter in itself indifferent, but it is based on the nature of man as already bound by the law of God written on his heart, and Adam's hearty acquiescence necessarily follows. So the two states at creation and in paradise can be distinguished but not separated.

John Calvin (1509–64) insists that no reward is due to works of obedience apart from a covenant by God in which he graciously agrees to accept them. However, before the law of Moses was given there was no such covenant.[1] Calvin's understanding of Genesis 2:16–17 perhaps implicitly recognises a covenant, but he does not express it. A generation after his death it becomes explicit.

On the other hand, **Ursinus** defines law in a way requiring a reward for obedience: 'A Law in general is a sentence commanding that which is honest, and binding the reasonable creature to obedience, with a promise of reward if that obedience be performed, and threatening of punishment, if it be violated.'[2] On this view,

1 John Calvin, *The Epistles of Paul to the Galatians, Ephesians, Philippians and Colossians* [1548] translated by T.H.L.Parker (Edinburgh: Oliver and Boyd, 1965), 59 [on Gal 3:17].

2 Zachary Ursinus, *A Collection of Certain Learned Discourses* translated

the Law is already a kind of covenant, and Adam could have had the possibility of some kind of reward apart from the specifics of Genesis 2:16–17.

With the advent of the two-covenant scheme some clarity is achieved: there is a covenant with Adam and with humanity in him. However, those adhering to the classic two-covenant view do not always attain a satisfying clarity about the relationship between the state of creation and the covenant state of Genesis 2:16–17.[3] Indeed, even in the doctrinal conclusions of the Westminster Assembly there are some tensions on this (cf. page 80 above). The 17th century writers do not often speak of a creation covenant by linking the 'covenant with day and night' in Jeremiah 31/33 back beyond Noah's covenant in Genesis 9 to a covenantal creation in Genesis 1. Nor have I noted Genesis 6:18 interpreted as a *confirmation* of God's existing covenant (as the Hebrew term implies) rather than a *commencement* of that covenant.[4] The twin-covenant men link God's law in man's heart with the specific covenant of Genesis 2:16–17, and a clear affirmation of a covenant

---

from the Latin text of David Pareus by I.H. (London: J. Broome, 1600) 256 (italics in original); also Ans. 36 in his Major Catechism reproduced on page 56).

3 This is not unconnected with the question of the image of God, a larger question than can be covered in this monograph. Bucanus rightly saw the whole man as created after God's image—thus his soul, body, gifts, dignity and lordship, *Institutions of Christian Religion* (London, 1606) 100ff. Similarly, H. Bavinck, *Reformed Dogmatics*, Vol. 2, 554ff), but it was more common to think of the image only in terms of spiritual qualities which distinguished man from the other creatures and by which he knew God and his will.

4 William Perkins in *An Exposition of the Creede* in *Collected Works* (London 1605), 168 comes close on both points when he writes of the 'renewing' of the covenant with Noah in the context of describing the glory and majesty of man in his original creation as inferred from the relatively small measure of glory and majesty in Genesis 9. Calvin, *Commentary on Jeremiah*, does relate Jer. 33:20ff to the creation, and George Walker identifies the covenant of Jer. 33:20 with the covenant made with man in the creation (*The manifold wisdome*, 56–57).

state before the specifics seems lacking. Still, some writers do see at least an implicit covenant in man's created state in God's image.

Rollock (1597): 'The covenant of works, which may also be called a legal or natural covenant, is founded in nature, which was pure and holy, and in the law of God, which was in the first creation engraved in man's heart. For after God had created man after his own image, pure and holy, and had written his law in his mind, he made a covenant with man. In it he promised him eternal life upon the condition of good and holy works which should correspond to the holiness and goodness of their creation and conform to his law. That nature, thus beautified with holiness and righteousness, and the light of God's law, is the foundation of the covenant of works, is very clear. For a covenant on the condition of good works and perfect obedience to God's law could not well stand with the justice of God unless he had first created him pure and holy, and had engraved his law in his heart, from whence those good works might proceed.'[5] [Compare with John Downame below.]

Ball (1615): '*Were these things bestowed upon man that he might live as he list?* No, but that he might serve the Lord his Maker, who therefore gave him a law binding him always to perfect obedience, and a special commandment to try [test] him.'[6]

Ames (1623): '...since man is less perfect than the angels and needs more instruction and practice, something positive was added to (though of the same basis as) the law of nature...[and] because man in this animal life understands by the senses and is led by the hand, as it were, from sensible to intelligible and spiritual things,

5 Robert Rollock, *Treatise*, 6–7.

6 John Ball, *A Short Treatise contayning all the Principall Grounds of Christian Religion, by way of questions and answers...* (Cambridge, 1615), citation from the 4th edition (London: Thomas Pauier, 1624), 66.

outward symbols and sacraments were added to the spiritual law to illustrate and confirm it. These symbols contained a special and positive law, a profession of general obedience to the law of nature put in man before, and a solemn confirmation of promises and threats as sanctions.'[7]

John Downame (c. 1628): 'For this Covenant [of works] requires works done by the strength of Nature, and according to the Law of our Creation, answerable to God's justice, the express image whereof is in the Moral Law. And therefore the nature of Men and Angels, beautified in their first creation with Holiness, and the Light of God's Law written in their heart, is the ground and foundation of this Covenant, for otherwise it could not have stood with the justice of God, to require these things at their hands, unless the Law of God had been stamped and signed in them, and their nature made holy and pure, able by Creation to do the same.'[8]

Leigh (1633): '...the foundation of the covenant of nature is the creation of man and the integrity of human nature.'[9]

Fisher (1645) holds that the law written on the heart, the moral law, was the matter of the covenant of works, but did not have the form of a covenant until the specific agreement of Genesis 2:16–17. Adam would have lived by the moral law apart from the covenant, but it is the covenant that provides for 'judgment, discretion and election' in decision making, appropriate recognition of God's sovereignty and a means by which man might receive blessing by God's 'gift and gentleness'.[10]

---

7 William Ames, *The Marrow*... 112–113.

8 John Downame, *The Summe of Sacred Divinitie*, 223.

9 Edward Leigh, *A Treatise*... 68.

10 Edward Fisher, *The Marrow*... (1st ed) 7–11; in 2nd ed. (1646) Chapter 1 (pages 27–32 in the edition with Boston's notes).

Strong (d. 1654): '...God dealt with man in a Covenant way in his Creation. Man stands bound to God by a double bond of Creation and stipulation; the one is natural and necessary, and the other voluntary. Thus God binds the Creature to himself by all imaginable engagements, to prevent future apostasy. By the one we are bound to God, and by the other God is bound to us.'[11]

Roberts (1657): 'that God in writing the moral law in Adam's heart, entered into a covenant of works with him, viz: by real impressions upon his heart, though not by verbal impressions to his ear. For by the law written in Adam's heart, he had laid before him what obedience was required, and assented to on Adam's part, and what recompense should be performed on God's part. And so this was at least an implicit if not an explicit covenanting.'[12]

Sedgwick (d. 1658): 'The Covenant of works (as to our part) was founded upon the strength of the righteous nature which God gave unto Adam, and in him unto us; so that his standing was upon his own bottom, upon the sufficiency of his own power and will, with which he was created.'[13]

---

11 William Strong, *A Discourse*... 1–2.

12 Francis Roberts, *Mysterium and Medulla*... 20–21.

13 Obadiah Sedgwick, *The Bowels of Tender Mercy*, 9.

12

THE PURPOSE OF THE PROBATION COMMAND

The specific probation command put the choice of God's authority or man's opinion before Adam in crystal clear form, and thus amounted to a test of Adam's attitude to the entire moral law written on his heart, and to God as its author.

Ball (1615): 'God the Creator of man, and in that respect his supreme and absolute sovereign, having bestowed so great gifts and main liberties upon man freely, might upon his own will and pleasure require at the hands of man what obedience soever he had, or would enable him to perform, and might also enjoin him to manifest his loyalty and humility, by abstaining from some act in itself indifferent, for no other reason but because he was so commanded.'[1]

Ball (d. 1640): 'The obedience which God required at his hands was partly natural—to be regulated according to the Law engraved in the heart by the finger of God himself—consisting in the true unfeigned and perfect love of God, and of his Neighbour for the Lord's sake; and partly symbolical, which stood in obedience to the law given for his probation and trial, whether he would submit

1 John Ball, *A Short treatise*, 66.

to the good pleasure of God in an act of itself merely indifferent, because he was so commanded.'[2]

Wollebius (1626): 'If all aspects of this sin [of Adam] are taken into account, it is rightly called transgression of the entire natural law.'[3]

Burgess (1657): 'Why God would give a positive law, besides that of the natural Law in his heart. There are these reasons commonly given: (1) That hereby God's dominion and power over man might be acknowledged...Adam in this was not to consider the greatness or goodness of the matter, but the will of the commander... (2) That so Adam's obedience might be the more tried and be manifested to be obedience...so that the forbearing to eat was not from any sin in the action but from the will of the law-giver.'[4]

Barret (1675): 'To the unchangeable Law of Nature, God (our sovereign Lord) may add what Positive Laws his Divine Wisdom judges meet, whereby to try his creature's obedience. And there is no positive precept of his given to Man, but Man is immediately bound to obey it; even by the Law of Nature, which requires this in general, that we obey God in all things.'[5]

Coxe (1681) '...Adam was set in his way but not actually brought to his eternal rest in that state wherein which he was created; being capable of, and made for, a greater degree of happiness than he immediately enjoyed, which was set before him as the reward of his obedience by that Covenant wherein he was to walk with God...'[6]

---

2 John Ball, *A Treatise of the Covenant of Grace*, 10.

3 Johannes Wollebius, *Compendium Theologiae Christianae* translated by J.W. Beardslee, *Reformed Dogmatics* (Grand Rapids: Baker, 1965) IX. 6 (p. 68).

4 Anthony Burgess, *Vindiciae Legis*, 106.

5 John Barret, *Good Will Towards Men*, 35.

6 Nehemiah Coxe, *A Discourse of the Covenants*, 25.

13

NOT ADDING WHAT IS LACKING BUT CONFIRMING WHAT IS GIVEN

The covenant of works is not to be viewed as the addition of supernatural qualities to the man of nature, as in traditional Roman Catholic theology, which supernatural qualities were then lost in the fall. Rather, it is a means by which God may crown the creature made in his image with glory and honour such as could not be attained by him in any other way.

Rollock (1597): 'God made this covenant of works with man as one friend does with another, for in the creation we were God's friends and not his enemies...The thing promised in the covenant is life eternal first, not righteousness: for that man in his creation was even then just and perfect...'[1]

Ball (d. 1640): '...the Covenant is of God, and that of his free grace and love...This Covenant was made in Justice; yet so it was of Grace likewise to make such a free promise, and to bestow such great things upon man [in return] for his obedience.'[2]

Burgess (1647): '...when God enters into a covenant or promise, you must conceive of this promise suitably to his great majesty...as

1 Robert Rollock, *A Treatise*... 7.
2 John Ball, *A Treatise*... 9.

a merciful condescension on God's part to promise such things to us, that so we might be the more confirmed in our hope in him... [Another reason for God issuing a threat might be] 'to incite and encourage Adam the more to obedience...And here you may see that to do a duty because of a reward promised is not a slavish and unlawful thing, for did not God deal thus with Adam?...Will you say with the Antinomian, that this is an unlawful thing, and this was to make Adam legal, and one that was not affected by the goodness of God to him? It is true, if a man obey God out of love to anything more than God, or equally with God, this is unlawful..... Adam was not able to obey any command of God, without the help of God. Though some will not call it grace, because they suppose that only comes by Christ, yet all they that are orthodox do acknowledge a necessity of God's enabling Adam to do what was good, else he would have failed.'[3]

3 Anthony Burgess, *Vindiciae Legis*... 127,128,129.

14

THE LIFE PROMISED IN THE COVENANT

Some considered the life promised in the covenant of works to be merely the continuation of the earthly life Adam already enjoyed. Others were specific that the ultimately heavenly glorification was intended. There was no general agreement at the time of the Westminster Assembly, hence the question is not decided in the documents produced by it. However, by 1675 the consensus had moved and the *Helvetic Consensus* Canons 8, 9 (see Table 5) speak very definitely of heavenly life.

Bucanus (d. 1603): 'What then should have become of man in the conclusion if he had not sinned; should he have [for]ever lived upon the earth? No: but he should have in the end have removed into heaven, indeed without death (which is the dissolution of the soul from the body) but yet not without some change, such as the Apostle speaks of (I Cor 15:51) in the bodies of the elect, who shall be then living; at the coming of the Lord they shall remove hence into heaven.'[1]

Rollock (1597): '...for after the man had lived godly and justly according to God's law in that integrity, then he might be said to be just again, and to be declared by God to be just by his good

1 William Bucanus, *Institutions*, 111.

works well pleasing unto God, and so eternal life might be said to be given to him, as justified by his works.'[2]

Ball (1615): 'Q. Death we hear was threatened if he did disobey; what promise was made to encourage him in this duty? Ans. The continuance both of himself and his posterity, in that good estate, Gen. 2:9.'[3]

Ball (d. 1640): 'The good God promised was a perfect system of good, which was to be continued so long as he continued obedient...But upon a supposition of Adam's persisting in a state of obedience, to say God would have translated him to the state of glory in Heaven, is more than any just ground will warrant, because in Scripture there is no such warrant.'[4]

Ames (1623): 'Fifth, in the sanction of this law there was a promise of continuing animal life, a later exaltation to spiritual life...'[5]

Ussher compilation (1625/45): '*What is meant by life promised to those that should keep all the Commandments?* The reward of blessedness and everlasting life, Lev.18:5; Luke 10:28.'[6] [The context of this statement is not limited to the post-fall situation.]

John Downame (c. 1628): 'The reward as we heard is life: He that does these things, shall live by them (Lev. 18:5; Ezek. 20:11; Rom. 10:5; Gal. 3:12). Life, the greatest good that can possibly come unto a creature, the full blessedness and perfection of his nature: for by it is meant a continuance, with growth and increase

2 Robert Rollock, *A Treatise*, 10.
3 John Ball, *A Short Treatise*, 67.
4 John Ball, *A Treatise on the Covenant*, 10.
5 William Ames, *Marrow*, I.X.31 (p.113).
6 James Ussher, *A Body of Divinitie*, 125.

in all Holiness, Happiness, immortality. And what more sweet than Life, wherein all Pleasures are enjoyed.'[7]

Fisher (1645): '...If Adam had continued obedient then had all mankind not only continued their animal life but should afterwards have been exalted to a spiritual and eternal life, for inasmuch as man was the head and chief of all earthly creatures, and so in regard to degrees next to God, so if he had continued obedient, God would have communicated himself more immediately unto him: for it is the glory of the Creator to communicate himself to the Creature; for indeed, the top and spire of that perfection which all mankind should have attained unto was the enjoyment of God immediately, which was indeed eternal life.'[8] [In subsequent editions, this section is omitted. It would have appeared on page 32 in the common editions with Boston's notes. This omission suggests the influence of discussions in 1645, which apparently tended to hesitate on the nature of the promised life.]

Burgess (1647) is agnostic. He writes: 'And this must be said, that we must not curiously start questions about that state in innocency; for the Scripture, having related that there was such a state once, doth not tell us what would have upon supposition of his obedience.'[9]

Bulkeley (1651): '[The covenant of works and the covenant of grace] agree in this, that in both there is a promise of life and blessedness; the Covenant of works saith, *Do this and live*; the covenant grace saith, *Believe and live*. Life is promised in both. Now whether the same life be promised in both, or whether a terrene

7 John Downame, *The Summe of Sacred Divintie*, 225–226.
8 Edward Fisher, *The Marrow,* 1st ed. 1645, 11–12.
9 Anthony Burgess, *Vindiciae*, 136.

[earthly] felicity and life here on earth, be promised in the one, and an heavenly in the other, as some think, or whether a heavenly life and glory in both, as some others think, I will not determine, it not being much material. It's enough to know that life and blessedness was and is promised in both.'[10]

Rutherford (1655): 'Communion with God in glory, is a reward not due by nature, but by the free gift of God to the most perfect law obedience...But that Adam should have such an eminent life for the reward of his obedience as communion with God, which is far above his obedience, is the free donation of God...'[11]

Roberts (1657): '*Q. What life it was which God further promised Adam upon his persisting in obedience.* Ans. 1. It seems clear that not only a *temporary life*, only for some limited time, was promised *Adam*; but even an Eternal life, without end, in the case of obedience. Forasmuch as not only temporal but also Eternal Death was threatened to *Adam*, and inflicted upon his posterity for disobedience. 2. But whether *Adam* should have enjoyed this Eternal Life still in the earthly Paradise, or should after some certain time have been translated and taken up into the Heavenly Paradise, that is by some disputed. Yet (1) *seeing* Scripture is silent touching any such translations, and (2) *seeing* that the giving of the Heavenly Paradise is the prerogative of Christ the *Last Adam,* the *Heavenly Adam*, as the Earthly Paradise came by the *First* and the *Earthly Adam*, it would argue too much temerity to determine upon it. This is certain, his everlasting life would have been a most sweet and happy life with God.'[12]

---

10 Peter Bulkeley, *The Gospel-covenant*, 55.

11 Samuel Rutherford, *The Covenant of Life Opened*, 22.

12 Francis Roberts, *Mysterium*, 27; see also Anthony Burgess, *Vindiciae*, 107–108.

Bridge (1667): '...God did enter into Covenant with Adam, and so with us, and promised eternal life in Heaven; not eternal life in this World only, as some would: for Hell was threatened in these words, in the day thou eatest thereof thou shalt die the death, and therefore Heaven and salvation was promised on the contrary...'[13]

13 William Bridge, *Christ and the Covenant*, 61, who quotes the Geneva Bible.

15

WHAT WAS THE NATURE OF THE DEATH THREATENED?

The early Reformed writers did not regard Adam as endowed with an essentially immortal body before the fall. Rather, Adam possessed a body of the earth, which was kept from harm by the providence of God, and from death by God's grace.

Bucanus (1605) is typical: 'that it [Adam's body] could die it had from the condition of nature, for it was taken out of the watery earth...according to that *Thou art dust* (Gen. 3:19) and therefore by nature mortal. But in that it was immortal, or had power not to die, it was not from the constitution of nature, but by the benefit of grace, because God granted this grace to man that he had power not to die, if he would have obeyed his commandments... the providence of God and the custody of angels did watch against all hurtful things...'[1]

Among Socinians, and some Arminians, the threat to Adam was regarded as that of bodily death not eternal death.[2] The Reformed held that temporal and eternal death, together with the miseries of this life, were the clear results of sin and involved in the death threatened.

1 William Bucanus, *Institutions* (London, 1606), 110.

2 Note H. Witsius, *Economy*, I. V, 88ff. who critiques the views of Etienne de Courcelles (1586–1659), professor of theology at the college of the Remonstrants.

Citing Genesis 2:17, **John Downame** (c. 1628) writes: 'Death therefore is the reward of sin: Death both spiritual in a subjection to the power of sin, and real, in an estate subject to destruction. Thus the Apostle Paul doth expound it (Eph. 2:1–3) when he teaches, that by nature we are first, *dead in sin, the sons of disobedience* and then *the children of wrath and condemnation*.'[3]

In the compilation by **James Ussher** (1625/45) it is put summarily: '*What is meant by death threatened to those that should transgress?* In this world the curse of God and death with manifold miseries both of body and soul, and (where this curse is not taken away) everlasting death both of body and soul in the world to come, Deut. 27:26; 29:19–20; 32:22. Leviticus 26; Deut. 28.'[4]

The **Shorter Catechism** of the Westminster Assembly (1647) reads: Q.19 *What misery did the fall bring upon mankind?* Ans. The fall brought upon mankind loss of communion with God, and his wrath and curse, so that we are justly made liable to all miseries in this life, to death itself, and to the pains of hell for ever.

The question of some as to why the punishment of death was not carried out immediately as apparently threatened ['*in the day that you eat you will surely die*'] had received various answers. The Reformed rejected the rabbinical opinion that, as a day with the Lord is as 1000 years, Adam did die in the day he sinned since he reached only 930 years (Gen. 5:5).[5] **Roberts** (1657) expresses the common viewpoint when he says that Adam immediately died

3 John Downame, *The summe of sacred divinitie* (London, c. 1628), 226.

4 James Ussher, *A Body of divinitie* (London 1645), 125.

5 E.g. Francis Roberts, *Mysterium*, 29; H. Witsius, *Economy*, 83. It is worth noting that the grammatical form of Genesis 2:16 is the form used for divine or royal edicts (cf. Gen. 20:7), and so means, 'You shall surely die at my hands'. It also stresses the certainty of death, not when it will happen (cf. 1 Kings 2:37,42).

spiritually, while his body immediately came under sentence of death. 'He that before his fall had an ability of not dying, after his fall brought upon himself an impossibility of not dying.' Finally, he became liable immediately to eternal death in body and soul.

16

THE SIGNIFICANCE OF THE TREES IN PARADISE

When the trees in the Garden are discussed the Reformed everywhere reject the idea that the tree of life had the inherent ability through God's provision to preserve man's life if he ate of it from time to time. Turretin writes: '...it cannot thence be rightly inferred that there was a physical power in this tree of so great efficacy that it could (its fruit being once tasted) rescue even sinful man from mortality. These words (Genesis 3:22) denote only the cause of his ejection from paradise on account of sin (by which, as by his own fault, he had cut himself off from that life, which was the thing signified). Thus he ought no longer to have any right to its sacrament.'[1]

While Rollock and Ball do not refer to the tree of life, **Polanus**, in his *Syntagma*, regards both trees as sacramental, one of life, the other of death, and is followed by Ames and Wollebius, Ussher, Leigh and most other Puritans, as also Turretin.[2] **Bucanus** speaks only of the tree of life as sacramental, representing that which,

1 Francis Turretin, *Institutes* I, 581.

2 Amandus Polanus, *Syntagma*, VI.50; William Ames, *Marrow*, I. X.33; Wollebius, *Compendium*, trans. Beardslee, VIII.1.ii-v (p.64), James Ussher, *A Body of Divintie*, 125; similarly Ussher, *The Principles*, 65; Francis Turretin, *Institutes*, I, 579, 581.

by the promise of God, would be his if he continued obedient to God's commands.[3]

Leigh (1633): 'The two Sacraments of this Covenant were the Tree of knowledge, respecting the Law, *do this*, and the tree of life respecting the promise, *Live*.'[4]

Strong (d. 1654): 'In the Covenant God made with *Adam* there was a Life promised, of which the Tree of life was a Seal; and there was a Death threatened, which was sealed by the Tree of Knowledge of God and Evil. In the threatening, *Thou shalt die*, the Promise is implied, *This do and thou shalt live*; and therefore the one is called the *Sacrament of Life*, and the other the *Sacrament of Death*.'[5]

In **Cocceius** (1648) two sacraments of the covenant of works are identified: (a) paradise itself as a pledge of the heavenly city and (b) the tree of life as a pledge of eternal life. **Witsius** included also the tree of knowledge of good and evil, and added the sabbath as a pledge of the blessed rest with God in the heavenly city. It has been said that later the usual position was to omit the tree of knowledge of good and evil if only because a sacrament consists of the use of natural things to represent spiritual benefits, and the use of the tree of knowledge of good and evil was forbidden.[6]

---

3 William Bucanus, *Institutions*, 111. Turretin says (*Institutes*, I, 584) that Christ is called the tree of life [in Revelation] because he restores that promise of life to us which this tree sealed to our first parents.

4 Edward Leigh, *A Treatise*, 64.

5 William Strong, *A Discourse*, 1.

6 Hermann Witsius, *Economy*, I.vi.ii (p.105); cf. H. Heppe, *Reformed Dogmatics* [German 1861; English translation by G.T.Thomson] (London: George Allen & Unwin, 1950) 296–298 for illustration of the variety of viewpoint.

17

THE QUESTION OF GRACE AND MERIT

While the term *grace* has come to be used in evangelical theology for redemptive grace, some parts of the New Testament use it without any notion of favour in the presence of demerit (e.g. Luke 1:30; 2:53; Acts 2:47). It is widely used in this more general sense in the 17th century Calvinistic writers.

Various writers, drawing on earlier medieval discussions, so stress God's freedom and sovereign will (*potentia absoluta*), that the fact it is the will of God, whose nature is holy, righteous, wise and good, moves somewhat into the background. Dr **William Twisse** (c. 1578–1646), a member of the Westminster Assembly, and a Calvinist of international standing, even went so far as to argue that, apart from his covenant, God's freedom was such that he could have forgiven sin without satisfaction. This kind of reasoning, a minority position, was represented in his Scottish disciple Samuel Rutherford. Such an emphasis is rejected with horror by Witsius in 1677, as it was in Cocceius before him (1648).[1] The general position of the 17th century Reformed Confessions

1 On Rutherford see J. Walker, *The Theology and Theologians of Scotland* [1888] (repr. Edinburgh: Knox Press, 1982), 8–13, 67–70. For Witsius, *The Ecomomy..*, Vol. 1, 78; cf. J. Cocceius, *Summa Doctrinae de Foedere*, 43, 170, as cited in S. Strehle, *Calvinism, Federalism and Scholasticism* (Bern: Peter Lang, 1988), 226.

is infralapsarian, and a generic consensus Calvinism, in which the will of God reflects his character.

Nevertheless, the notion of merit is universally rejected by Reformed writers. Thus **Perkins**: 'I. We renounce all personal merits, that is, all merits within the person of any mere man. II. And we renounce all merit of works, that is, all merit of any work done by any mere man whatsoever... [And as regards even Adam] if he had stood to this day, he could not by his continual and perfect obedience, have procured a further increase of favour at God's hand, but should only have continued that happy state in which he was first created.'[2]

Grace in regard to the covenant of works was recognised at several points, as noted in (1) to (5) following:

1. God was not obligated to create humanity in the first place, a point universally accepted as axiomatic.
2. God was not bound to enter into covenant with humanity. That he did so was of his undeserved kindness and grace. Many writers affirming this view hold that God could have left man in the state of nature without a covenant of works, and terminated his existence at his pleasure. However, he made a covenant of works with humanity in order to provide a blessing otherwise unobtainable. That he did so involves a voluntary and gracious condescension. This seems to be the usual position until the time of Westminster (cf. WCF 7:1).

Rollock (1597): 'It is a question here, whether in the first creation, good works in the covenant of works, were required of

---

2 William Perkins, *A Reformed Catholike* [1597] in *Collected Works* (London 1605), 690.

man as meritorious for the promised life? I answer, not so. But they were due in the creation as pledges of thankfulness in man to his creator, for that excellent work of his creation, and to glorify God his creator.' Thus Rollock holds the necessity of obedience, but denies it deserved or merited the promised life.

The 'learned Doctor' **William Ames** (1623) states: 'In this covenant the moral deeds of the intelligent creature lead either to happiness as a reward or to unhappiness as a punishment. The latter is deserved the former not.'[3]

John Downame (c. 1628): 'But see the exceeding bounty and goodness of God, that will not have us serve him for naught. He is pleased for the perfect keeping of his Law, and the Righteousness by him enjoined, not only to promise a recompense of reward, but to contract and covenant with us, and under certain conditions as it were, to bind himself unto it, which is the same that we call the Law or Covenant of works...'[4]

John Ball (d. 1640) stresses that, apart from the covenant, God in justice owed even an obedient Adam nothing. It is because of the covenant with its gracious provision that reward is due in justice, ie. because God has pledged himself. His pledge could have been on other less favourable terms, hence God showed his goodness as well as his justice.

Ball writes: 'The Covenant is of God, and that of his free grace and love. For although in some covenants the good covenanted be promised in justice and given in justice for our works, yet it was of grace that God was pleased to bind himself to his creature, and above the desert of the creature; and though the reward be of

3 William Ames, *The Marrow*, translated by J.D.Eusden, I.X.11 (p. 111).
4 John Downame, *The Summe of Sacred Divinitie*, 223.

justice it is also of favour. For after perfect obedience performed according to the will of God, it had been no injustice in God, as he made the creature of nothing, so to have brought him unto nothing. It was then of grace that he was pleased to make that promise, and of the same grace his happiness should have been continued.... God did in justice proportion the reward and the work, the weight of the blessing promised, and the work of obedience required. But yet I cannot think that it had been injustice in God to have given less, or not to have continued so great things to man, so long as he continued his obedience.'[5]

Burgess (1647): 'Yet though it were a Covenant of works, it cannot be said to be of merit. Adam, though in innocency, could not merit that happiness which God would bestow upon him. First, *because the enjoying of God, in which Adam's happiness did consist, was such a good as did far exceed the power and ability of man.* It's an infinite good, and all that is done by us is finite. And then in the next place, *Because even then Adam was not able to obey any command of God without the help of God.* Though some will not call it grace, because they suppose that only comes by Christ, yet all they that are orthodox do acknowledge a necessity of God's enabling Adam to that which was good, else he would have failed. Now then, if by the help of God Adam was strengthened to do the good he did, he was so far from meriting thereby, that indeed he was the more obliged to God.'[6]

Burgess urges his readers to thankfulness for God's dealing by covenant: 'There is no natural or Moral necessity that God should do thus. We are his, and he might require obedience without

5 John Ball, *A Treatise on the Covenant,* 7.
6 Anthony Burgess, *Vindiciae*, 129.

any covenanting. But yet, to show his love and goodness, he condescends to this way...Was then eternal life and happiness a mere gift of God to Adam for his obedience and love? What a free and mere gift then is salvation and eternal life to thee? If Adam was not to put any trust in his duties, if he could not challenge God for a reward, how then shall we rely upon our performances, that are so full of sin?'[7]

Dickson/Durham, *Sum of Saving Knowledge* (1650): '[God] made our first parents, Adam and Eve, the root of mankind, both upright and able to keep the law written in their heart. Which law they were naturally bound to obey under pain of death; but God was not bound to reward their service, till he entered into a covenant or contract with them, and their posterity in them, to give them eternal life, upon condition of perfect personal obedience; withal threatening death in case they should fail. This is the covenant of works.'[8]

Rutherford (1655): 'Communion with God in glory, is a reward not due by nature, but by the free gift of God to the most perfect law obedience...But that Adam should have such an eminent life for the reward of his obedience as communion with God, which is far above his obedience, is the free donation of God nor is there any necessary connection between Adam's perfect obedience and so high and eminent a life, nor can this Covenant, as touching such a promise, be written in his heart. God then never loved to make any Covenant, yea even that of Works, without some acts and out-goings of grace, and this hire was grace; how is he not to be served who loves to hire and allure us to be happy.'[9]

7 Anthony Burgess, *Vindiciae*, 131; similarly Francis Roberts, *Mysterium*, 23.
8 *The Sum of Saving Knowledge II.* For the full text see page 86.
9 Samuel Rutherford, *The Covenant of Life Opened*, 22.

Patrick Gillespie (1661): 'Both the covenant of works and the covenant of grace 'agree in this, that there was very much of grace and favour in both. The *moving cause* in both was mere Grace, although the last has the honour by way of eminency to be styled the Covenant of Grace (whereof in its place) yet even the Covenant of Works (howsoever the condition of it was obedience, and the reward of it was to works), even that Covenant was thus far a Covenant of Grace.'[10]

Bridge (1667): Writing of the new covenant, Bridge says: 'New in opposition to the Covenant that was made with Adam in the state of innocency; for then, God out of free love and grace, was pleased to condescend to enter into Covenant with man, yet then God dealt with us in a way of *Supremacy* and of *Righteousness*; and therefore there is mention made only of the *Threatening*, In the day that thou eatest thereof, thou shalt die the death. But now God deals with us in a way of grace, and of great compassion; and therefore in this covenant there is mention made only of the Promise.'[11]

3. Alternatively to (2), the covenant (of works, not of grace) was necessary, a reality flowing from the nature of God. The character of God is such that he cannot withhold his love and all its effects from a holy and innocent creature made in his image. God is love and it is the nature of love to seek union and communion with the beloved. On this view it is still gracious of God to create humanity knowing that the necessity of his nature would require self-giving in covenant

10 Patrick Gillespie, *The Ark of the Testament Opened*, 221.
11 William Bridge, *Christ and the Covenant*, 61. Bridge quotes the Geneva Bible.

to the holy creature. This seems the view prevalent in such as Cocceius and Witsius.

Witsius (1677): 'I lay this down as an acknowledged truth, that God owes nothing to his creature. By no claim, no law is he bound to reward it. For all that the creature is, it owes entirely to God; both because he created it, and also, because he is infinitely exalted above it...Whatever then is promised to the creature by God, ought all to be ascribed to the immense goodness of the Deity...Nor can God on account of this his goodness refuse to communicate himself to, or give the enjoyment of himself to, an innocent, an holy creature...He does not love in reality, who desires not to communicate himself to the object of his affection...The sum of the divine commands is ...love me above all things...But how is it conceivable that God should thus speak to the soul, and the soul should religiously attend to, and diligently perform this, and yet never enjoy God...[for God to say] "long after me, but on condition, never of obtaining thy desire..."'[12]

'The promises therefore of the covenant contain greater things than this communion or fruition of God, of whatsoever kind it be, which Adam already enjoyed whilst still in the state of trial. A farther degree of happiness, consisting in the full and immediate enjoyment of God, and in a more spiritual state, to last for ever, was proposed to him, which the scripture usually sets forth under the title of eternal life. And this is the proper question; whether the promise of eternal life, to be entered upon by all after a complete course of obedience, flows from the natural goodness of God, or, whether it be of free and liberal good pleasure?' [Witsius inclines to the former and concludes] 'Lord, we know thou art indebted

12 Herman Witsius, *The Economy of the Covenants*, Vol. 1, 76–79.

to none, and that there is none who can say to thee, what dost thou, or why dost thou? That thou art holy, and infinitely good, and therefore a lover and rewarder of holiness. May the consciousness of our ignorance in other things kindle in our hearts an ineffable desire of that beatific vision, by which, knowing as we are known, we may in the abyss of thy infinity behold those things which no thought of ours at present can reach.'[13]

4. Whatever view out of (2) or (3) was taken, the reward is always of God's goodness and the language of merit, in the sense of earning/deserving the reward, is held to be inappropriate. It is a reward deriving from God's promise in the covenant, and in that sense absolutely just, but it does not arise from any intrinsic worth (*condign* merit) that corresponds to the reward as if wages paid for services rendered. Nor is the obedience to be thought of as acquiring *congruent* merit, that is, merit not truly adequate but accepted as sufficient. The universal Reformed position recognised God's abundant goodness in his covenant promise. God would reward humanity not because we deserved it but because of his goodness and his faithfulness to his covenant pledge. The distinction between merit as meaning something obtained and merit as meaning reward due for the intrinsic worth of something should be kept in view; the former is acceptable, the latter not.[14]

The colourful preacher **Obadiah Sedgwick** (d. 1658), speaking of the differences between the two covenants, says: 'The covenant

---

13 Herman Witsius, *The Economy of the Covenants*, Vol. 1, 80–82.

14 Francis Turretin, *Institutes*, Vol. 2, 710–711. Note P. Gillespie, *The Ark* (1661), 198: 'Though Justice had some place in this Covenant, yet merit had none at all…Merit had as little place in man's integrity as demerit…'

of works, if we could attain unto it, would now be matter of glorying in ourselves.' After citing Romans 4:2, Luke 15:29 and Luke 17:10, also Romans 4:4, he adds: 'You might have earned happiness, if I may so speak, at your fingers' ends, and might have demanded your wages after you had done your work.'[15] This is a construction that suggests that Adam was created to be a legitimate Pharisee! It is an anomaly in the Puritan and Reformed tradition and possibly reflects a rhetorical flourish on the popular preacher's part as well as failure on Sedgwick's part to distinguish perfect Adam, full of love for God, from those who live post-fall.

Turretin (1679): 'There was no debt (properly so called) from which man could derive a right, but only a debt of fidelity, arising out of the promise by which God demonstrated his infallible and immutable constancy and truth. If the apostle seems to acknowledge this right or debt (Rom. 4:4), it must be understood in no other than a respective sense; not as the proportion and condignity of the duty rendered by God to man, (Rom. 8:18; Luke 17:10), but to the pact of God and justice (i.e., the fidelity of him making it).'[16]

5. <u>God gave sufficient grace to Adam for him to keep the covenant if Adam willed so</u>. **Bucanus** (d. 1603) writes: '*Did Adam besides these sound faculties stand in need of God's grace?* He did, whereby namely he might be preserved in that his integrity of nature, and might be furthered to those actions... But what kind of grace was that? Such a one, whereby if he would he was able to live holily, yet not whereby he would perpetually and constantly cleave to God; for if he had

15 Obadiah Sedgwick, *The Bowels of Tender Mercy*, 11–12.
16 Francis Turretin, *Institutes*, Vol. 1, 578, cf. Vol. 2, 712.

> received this grace undoubtedly he had persevered. ...Adam had received grace whereby he was able, if he would, not to sin, but he had not received grace whereby he would not, nor could not, sin.'[17]

William Pemble (1591–1623) notes: '*God gave Adam what strength he had...*'[18]

William Twisse (d. 1646): 'We say that Adam had sufficient grace to enable him to obey the law given to him; we deny that he had efficacious grace which would cause him actually to obey the law. That he had the power to obey the law and that it could not happen that the law should be obeyed, are not contradictory; just as the soldiers were not deficient in the power to break the bones of the Saviour, yet the decree of God in opposition being posited, they could not be broken.'[19]

Anthony Burgess (1647) states: 'Adam was not able to obey any command of God, without the help of God. Though some will not call it grace, because they suppose that only comes by Christ, yet all they that are orthodox do acknowledge a necessity of God's enabling Adam to do what was good, else he would have failed.'[20]

Let **Patrick Gillespie** summarise: '(1) Grace and Favour in God, and nothing in man, gave the rise to that covenant [of Works], and to God's condescension to enter in to it. (2) Grace in God which freely endued man with all the habits of grace in perfection, made him fitted and able to have kept that Covenant which God made with him, for his absolute Sovereign owed him no more than

17 William Bucanus, *Institutions*, 108–109.

18 William Pemble, *Vindici Fidei* (Oxford: Edward Forrest, 1629) 64.

19 Guilielmi Twissi...*ad Jacobi Arminii Collationem cum Francisco Junio* (1649), 68 cited from Francis Turretin, *Institutes*, Vol. 1, 611.

20 Anthony Burgess, *Vindiciae Legis*...129.

the rest of the creatures which he had made. (3) Grace engaged by promise, the reward that was promised to works of obedience by that Covenant, for there was no merit in Adam's obedience nor in ours (Luke 17:10)... Neither did God owe any thing as debt for the obedience of man; his service was but an homage done to God, and no profit redounded to him by it, nor did his work bear proportion to the eternal reward promised for it.'[21]

21 Patrick Gillespie, *The Ark* (1661), 221.

18

THE RELATIONSHIP OF THE COVENANT OF WORKS TO THE SINAI COVENANT

If the repeated emphasis in Moses on obedience as necessary to blessing made the Sinai covenant look like a covenant of works, yet it was given to the redeemed people of God to be kept in gratitude (Exod. 20:1–2), and was attested in Scripture as not disannulling the earlier promise to Abraham (cf. Exod. 2:24–25; Exod. 6:4ff.; Gal. 3:17). How were these facts to be related? Working through the issue was complex. The intra-trinitarian covenant of redemption as the foundation of the covenant of grace was not generally distinguished before the 1640s, nor was the historical unfolding of the covenants and their inter-relatedness well perceived in the early period. As the subject was discussed there were different ways of defining a covenant in relation to law and promise, which added to the difficulty.

The 16th century Reformers, followed by the 17th century Puritan/Reformed writers, considered that the covenant with Moses and Israel could not be a covenant of works despite the ten commandments being a summary of the moral law given man in creation. To suppose the law of Moses temporarily or permanently established salvation for the Jews on the obedience-inheritance principle was an impossibility since the fall of our first parents. The law could not give life. Further, the law of Moses could not change the covenant of grace made with Abraham 430 years before. 'For if the inheritance depends on the law, then it no longer depends on a promise; but God in his grace gave it to Abraham through a promise' (Gal. 3:18).

There was considerable diversity of expression as covenant thinking was thought through, but a large measure of agreement was reached and expressed in the Westminster Confession in 1647. We turn to look at representative statements of the relation of the covenant of works with Adam and the covenant with Moses. Amid their diversity of explanation I again emphasise that all reject the idea that Sinai introduces salvation by our works and all see it as serving the covenant of grace in some sense.

A covenant of works, law or nature but…

Some spoke of the Mosaic covenant as a covenant of works but qualified through consideration of the reasons God gave it. All also recognised it could be extracted from its context and misapplied to support works-righteousness.

In **Polanus** (1589) the covenant with Moses is a repetition of the covenant of works but not with a view to works-righteousness. 'The repetition of the covenant of works is made by God (Exod. 19:5; Deut. 5:2; 1 Kings 1:21; Heb. 8:9) and that chiefly for four causes.

- That God by all means might stir up men to perform obedience.

- That every mouth might be stopped, and all the world might be made subject to the condemnation of God for not performing perfect obedience (Rom. 3:19).
- That he might manifest man's sin and naughtiness [=wickedness] (Rom. 3:19–20; 7:7–11).
- That he might thrust us forward to seek to be restored to the covenant of grace (Gal 3:22; 5:23).'[1]

Bucanus (d. 1603) regards the covenant at Sinai as an administration of the covenant of grace. 'Yet we must note that the old Covenant is understood and called two ways: sometimes only in respect of Moses and his lawgiving it is called the covenant of the law, the functioning and establishing of whereof is described (Exod. 24); and sometimes to signify the covenant of grace or free covenant, in what manner it was made with Abraham and his posterity (Gen. 17:7).'[2]

In 1608 **John Cameron** advanced the thesis of two unconditional covenants (that with Noah and the new covenant promulgated in Christ' redemptive work) and three conditional covenants: the covenant of *nature* with Adam, the covenant of *grace* given in increasingly clarity of promise successively to Adam, the patriarchs and Israel; and a covenant *subservient* to the covenant of grace being the temporary Mosaic covenant.[3] They are conditional in the sense that all require a response to the covenant maker on the part of man.

---

1 Amandus Polanus, *The Substance*, 88.

2 William Bucanus, *Institutions*, 215.

3 See also page 107. Richard A. Muller, 'Divine Covenants, Absolute and Conditional: John Cameron and the Early Orthodox development of Reformed Covenant Theology' *Mid-America Journal of Theology* 17 (2006), 11–56 is a succinct survey (also available online).

William Ames (1623): Under Moses 'the form of administration of the covenant of grace gave some evidence of the covenant of works' from which the new covenant fulfilled in Christ 'is essentially different.'[4]

William Pemble (1625) speaks of the two administrations of the covenant of works—with Adam before the fall, and with the Israelites at Sinai. 'God entered into covenant with the Israelites, promising to be their God in bestowing upon them all the blessings of life and happiness upon condition that they would be his people, obeying all things that he had commanded. This condition they accepted, promising an absolute obedience: "All things which the Lord has said, we will do" (Exod. 19:8).' They also accepted the curse if they disobeyed (Deut. 27:26).

However, Pemble insists God did not intend that the Jews should obtain salvation by obedience to the law: 'God knew well enough that they were never able to keep their promise, and therefore it was not God's intention in this legal covenant with the Jews that any of them should ever attain justification and life by that means.' Citing Galatians 3:19, Pemble says God's intention was to convict of sin, restrain from sin, and to humble man to receive the gospel.[5]

Wollebius (1626): 'The law was given and inscribed within the first man, so that by his own obedience, if he willed, eternal life could follow; it is offered to fallen man in order that, lacking all faculty of fulfilling the law, he may fulfill it through Christ. (Rom. 10:4: "The end of the law is Christ, for justification, to him who believes."). Therefore the promulgation of the law to Israel on

4 William Ames, *The Marrow*, I.XXXIX.4, 206.
5 William Pemble, *Vidici Fidei* (1625), 40; second edition (1629), 64.

Mount Sinai was a very gracious act...'[6] because of its intention, although its demand was unrelenting.

John Preston (1629): 'The covenant of works runs in these terms, "Do this and thou shalt live, and I will be thy God." This was the covenant God made with Adam, and the covenant that is expressed by Moses in the moral law.'[7]

Edward Leigh (1633): 'The Old Testament [ie. the Mosaic covenant] is the Covenant of God which in types and shadows prefigured Christ to come and to be exhibited, and by virtue thereof, Life everlasting was given by faith in Christ that was to come...it shows what a man owes to God, and how he must be punished if he pay not the debt, whence it makes him look to a mediator, when he sees himself unable to either pay the one or endure the other.'[8]

Edward Fisher (1645) holds that the Sinai covenant was a renewal of the covenant of works but yet not given for the same purpose as the covenant with Adam. 'For God never appoints anything to an end to which it is utterly unsuitable or improper. Now the covenant of works by sin is become weak and unprofitable to the purpose of salvation, and therefore God never appointed it to that end....we are to know that the purpose of God in the covenant made with Abraham was to give life and salvation by grace and promise; and therefore his renewing of the covenant of works was not, neither could be, to give the same life and salvation by working, for then there would have been contradictions in the covenants... It was not added by way of ingrediency, as a part of the

6 Johannes Wollebius, *Compendium*, XIII (1) vii-viii, p.76.
7 John Preston, *The New Covenant*, 317.
8 Edward Leigh, *A Treatise*, 71–72.

covenant of grace... but it was added by way of subserviency and attendance the better to advance and make effectual the covenant of grace.'[9]

Samuel Bolton (1645), later a Westminster divine, is one who prefers Cameron's three covenant scheme, as does **Thomas Goodwin**.[10] Bolton describes it thus: 'The covenant of nature was that whereby God required from the creature as creature perfect obedience to all divine commandments, with promise of a blessed life in Paradise if man obeyed, but with the threat of eternal death if he disobeyed the command, the purpose of all this being to declare how virtue pleased, and sin displeased God. The covenant of grace was that whereby God promised pardon and forgiveness of sins and eternal life, by the blood of Christ, to all those that should embrace Christ, and this was purposed by God to declare the riches of his mercy. The subservient covenant, which was called the old covenant, was that whereby God required obedience from the Israelites in respect of the moral, ceremonial and judicial laws. Blessings in the land of Canaan were promised to obedience, and curses and miseries to those who broke the covenant, and all to this end, that God might encourage their hearts in the expectation of the Messiah to come.'[11]

Bolton seems to have thought the Mosaic covenant could not be regarded as a covenant of grace since as a covenant of grace it would still be binding whereas Scripture testifies that Moses' covenant is not now binding. 'If it is neither a covenant of works,

9 Edward Fisher, *Marrow*, 27–28 (in 2nd ed [1646] the material appears later in Chapter 2, Section 3 (pp. 62–63 in the edition with Boston's notes published in Philadelphia c. 1870).

10 Thomas Goodwin, *The Works of Thomas Goodwin* (ed. James Nichol) Vol. 6, 354.

11 Samuel Bolton, *The True Bounds*, 94–95 (Banner of Truth edition).

nor a covenant of grace, then must it of necessity be a third kind of covenant: and it must be such as does not stand in opposition to grace, nor is inconsistent with the covenant of grace, for if this be so, then God will have contradicted himself, overthrown his own purpose, and repented of his own promise which he had given before. Hence it is called a subservient covenant. It was given by way of subserviency to the gospel and a fuller revelation of grace; it was temporary, and had respect to God's blessing there, if and as Israel obeyed. It had no relation to heaven, for that was promised by another covenant which God made before the subservient covenant.'[12]

George Walker, also later a Westminster divine, spoke of the Mosaic covenant as a *mixed* covenant of works and of grace. The moral law or ten commandments 'was nothing else but a renewing of the old Covenant of works which God made with Adam in Paradise'.[13] The second part of the Mosaic covenant consisted of the Levitical laws, the tabernacle, ark and mercy seat, which were types of Christ, together with what was given in the plains of Moab as set down in Deuteronomy [see 29:2]. Concerning it, 'this was nothing else but a renewing of the covenant of grace which he [God] had made with their fathers, Adam, Abraham, Isaac and Jacob'.[14] This distinction was justified by appeal to Deuteronomy 4:13 where God's covenant is described as the ten commandments, and to Deuteronomy 29:2.

Walker states that the Mosaic covenant requires 'that a man should first endeavour to fulfil the whole law that thereby he may

12 Samuel Bolton, 99.

13 George Walker, *The manifold wisdom of God*, 128,136. Published in 1641 this book, according to the preface, was written in 1616.

14 George Walker, *The manifold wisdom of God,* 139.

be justified and live; and if he cannot do so, that then he should flee to sacrifices for sin, and in them, as in types, to Christ and his righteousness and obedience, that there he may find that which by the law he cannot obtain.'[15]

I have already noted on page 77, Calamy's *Two solemne Covenants Made Between God and Man*, published in February 1646, with its not altogether accurate comments on the diversity of opinion on the covenants. Samuel Bolton provides another taxonomy.[16] **Calamy**, a member of the Westminster Assembly, wrote: 'Some object and say that the Law at Mount Sinai was a covenant of grace, and others say it was a covenant of works, but I shall prove that it was neither, but only given to those that were in covenant as a rule of obedience, for so runs the preface, *I am the Lord thy God*, that is, by the covenant of grace made with Jesus Christ, and confirmed to *Abraham*, therefore *thou shalt have no other God but me...*'[17]

Given that the law at Sinai is expressly called a covenant, this position has to interpret the term in another than the ordinary sense.[18]

John Ball: The influential John Ball's posthumously published book on the covenants was issued about July 1645 as the Assembly

15 George Walker, *The manifold wisdom of God,* 132.

16 See J.V.Fesko, *The Theology of the Westminster Standards* (Wheaton, IL: Crossway, 2014) whose Chapter 5 provides an historical survey with the taxonomies of Bolton and Calamy on pages 147–148. Mark Jones in the collection of essays edited by Michael A. G. Haykin and Mark Jones, *Drawn into Controversie: Reformed Theological Diversity and Debates Within Seventeenth-Century British Puritanism* (Göttingen: Vandenhoeck & Ruprecht, 2011), 180–200, provides an historical survey and discussion of the two-covenant and three-covenant schemes.

17 Edmund Calamy, *Two solemne Covenants*, 8.

18 As does, for example, Wilhelmus à Brakel, *The Christian's Reasonable Service* (Dutch 1700; ET: Pittsburg: Soli Deo Gloria, 1994) 3:44 in rejecting the notion of the ten commandments as a covenant of works.

was entering on the topic and was highly regarded. Ball wrote: 'The Covenant which God made with Israel is called the Old Testament or the Law, not because it was first, as some suppose, but because it was to wax old, and to give place to the more excellent Covenant succeeding, and finally [was] to be abolished (Heb. 8:13). But here at the first we meet with a great difficulty, How and whether at all the Covenant of Grace was manifested by Moses?'[19]

Ball reviews a number of proposals:

1. 'Some make the Old and New Testament as the Covenant of works and grace, opposite in substance and kind, and not in degree alone, and that to introduce an unsound distinction, viz. of promise set against Covenant or Testament, as though God conferred Grace unto the Fathers only by promise and not by Covenant...'

2. 'Others make the Old Testament a Covenant subservient to the Covenant of Grace' a kind of modified covenant of works including the ceremonial law, to show what man owes to God but this opinion also is to 'make the old Covenant differ from the new in substance and kind and not in degree ...'

3. 'Most Divines hold the old and new Covenants to be one in substance and kind, to differ only in degrees, but in setting down the differences they speak so obscurely that it is hard to find how they consent with themselves.'

4. Several options are outlined by Ball which I summarise: In reconciling the seeming contrary elements in the old covenant, some affirm that the promise of life for perfect obedience to the heavy burden coexists with a covert promise of life under the condition of repentance and faith in the Messiah to come who is prefigured in the law. Others stress a two-

19 John Ball, *A Treatise on the Covenant of Grace*, 92–93.

> fold demand of the law: there is the promise of life for perfect obedience or death for the slightest disobedience (Deut. 27:26), but there is also a promise of blessing to those 'who do what they can to perform it'. The first demand is opposite to the covenant of grace being a covenant of works; the second demand is subservient to the covenant of grace. This is said to be illustrated by various circumstances in the giving of the ten commandments. Further, Paul abstracts the legal demand in Galatians 3 and Romans 4. Yet the difficulty is not resolved these ways. The covenant with Israel is one covenant not two, and is treated as such by the Apostles.[20]

Ball therefore concludes:

5. 'Some Divines hold that the old Testament, even the Law, as it was given on Mount Sinai, to be the Covenant of Grace for substance, though propounded in a manner fitting to the state of that people, time and condition of the Church. It was so delivered as it might serve to discover sin, drive the Jews to deny themselves and flee to the mercy of God revealed in Jesus; but it was given to be a rule of life to a people in Covenant, directing them how to walk before God in holiness and righteousness, that they might inherit the promises of grace and mercy. This I take to be the truth, and it may be confirmed by many and strong reasons out of the word of God.' Ball's marginal note reads: 'The Law was never given or made positive without the Gospel, neither is the Gospel now without the Law, although the old Testament be usually called the Law and the new Gospel: because the Law is predominant in the one and the Gospel in the other.'[21]

20 John Ball, *A Treatise*, summarising 93–103.

21 John Ball, *A Treatise*, 102; numbers in have been supplied.

A dispensation of the covenant of grace

What we may regard as the classic position on the two-covenant scheme is expressed in the **Westminster Confession**, Chapter 7: *Of God's Covenant with Man*, which was finalised in June 1646. The relevant section for our present purpose reads:

> v. This covenant [of grace] was differently administered in the time of the law, and in the time of the Gospel: under the law it was administered by promises, prophecies, sacrifices, circumcision, the paschal lamb, and other types and ordinances delivered to the people of the Jews, all foresignifying Christ to come; which were, for that time, sufficient and efficacious, through the operation of the Spirit, to instruct and build up the elect in faith in the promised Messiah, by whom they had full remission of sins, and eternal salvation; and is called the Old Testament.
>
> vi. Under the Gospel, when Christ, the substance, was exhibited, the ordinances in which this covenant is dispensed are the preaching of the Word, and the administration of the sacraments of Baptism and the Lord's Supper: which, though fewer in number, and administered with more simplicity, and less outward glory, yet, in them, it is held forth in more fullness, evidence, and spiritual efficacy, to all nations, both Jews and Gentiles; and is called the New Testament. There are not therefore two covenants of grace, differing in substance, but one and the same, under various dispensations.

It should be noted, therefore, that the Confession did not exclude views of the Mosaic covenant that saw an aspect illustrative of the works-inheritance principle in it as a part of its particular administration of the one covenant of grace, but does reject the idea that in essence it was a covenant of works. In Chapter 19 of the Confession a distinction is drawn between the moral law, the civil law and the ceremonial law, which will be discussed in chapter 25 of this book.

Comments by several writers after the Confession was finalised follow:

Bulkeley (1651): '...the Law [of Moses] though it contains the sum of the Covenant of works, yet was not delivered unto that people for this end, to stand between them as a Covenant of works by which they should be justified and live, but only as it was subservient and helpful unto them to attain the end of the former Covenant of grace, which God had made with them in their Fathers...(p.63)...[Its purpose was] to prepare them for Christ, and the Covenant of Grace...and to teach them how to walk and please God when they were entered into a new covenant with him.'[22]

David Dickson [1656] is a robust example of a usual 17th century assessment: 'There is another counterfeit, bastard covenant of works, of man's own devising, which a sinner, lying in his sins (unable to do what the Law commands, or to suffer what the Law, being broken, binds upon him) of his own head devises upon other conditions than God has set, and will have God to take his devised covenant instead of perfect obedience to the Law, that so he may be justified. Such was the Covenant, which the carnal Israelites made with God in the wilderness, and which their posterity did follow, turning the Covenant of Grace, whereunto God was calling them, into a Covenant of Works of their own framing. For the grace which was offered them in Christ under the veil of levitical types, figures and ceremonies, they turned into an external performance only of bare and dead ceremonies, and into a ministry of the letter

22 Peter Bulkeley, *The Gospel Covenant* (London, 1651), 63–64.

and death; for they did not take up Christ to be the end of the law for righteousness to everyone that believes in him ....'[23]

Roberts (1657) draws largely on Ball. He distinguishes four different opinions, advocating the last: 'The first holding, that the Law on Mount Sinai was given as a Covenant of Works, not of grace, (or of Faith, as I had rather style it). 2. The second holding, That it was a Mixed Covenant, Partly of Works, Partly of Grace. 3. The third holding, That it was not purely and properly either a Covenant of Nature or of Grace, but a Covenant Subservient to the Covenant of Grace, and preparing thereunto. 4. The fourth holding, That it was a Covenant of Grace for Substance, though propounded in an unusual way of terror and servile bondage, suitable to the people, time and state of the Church under age.'[24]

Turretin (1682) makes the same four points as Roberts in the same order and in similar language.[25] In his argument against the three-fold covenant position of Cameron and others Turretin makes the telling point: To say that the Sinai covenant subserved the covenant of grace is really to say 'that it was not a different covenant in species, but only a different mode of economy, adapted to the time, place and state of the persons.'[26]

---

23 David Dickson, T*herapeutica sacra* [Latin 1656] (Edinburgh, 1664) Book 1, Ch 5., 82–83. Mark W. Karlberg, *Covenant theology in Reformed Perspective* (Eugene, OR: Wipf & Stock Publishers, 2000) claims Dickson taught: 'As a punishment, God promulgated the law on Mount Sinai as a repetition of the Covenant of Works, though hypothetical in nature' (p. 33). This is not my reading; rather, the Judaisers perverted the law's intent so bringing judgment on themselves.

24 Francis Roberts, *Mysterium Bibliorum*, 738–739 cf. 759f

25 Francis Turretin, *Institutes of Elenctic Theology*, Vol. 2., 262.

26 Francis Turretin, *Institutes of Elenctic Theology*, Vol. 2., 267.

An excluded position

The Westminster Confession at 7.6 states: There are not therefore two covenants of grace, differing in substance, but one and the same, under various dispensations. This appears a specific exclusion of the idea of the Sinai covenant as a covenant of grace as held by **Tobias Crisp**. Crisp (1643) held that the covenant with Moses was not a different administration of the one covenant of grace nor a covenant of works, but a distinct covenant of grace from that made in Christ. It was 'weak, imperfect, unprofitable, disannulled' compared to the covenant of grace with Christ which was 'perfect, established, and makes the comers thereunto perfect' and to which Jeremiah 31:31 and Hebrews 8:6 refer.[27]

On the surface it does not appear that this position differs in substance from the classic view. However, for Crisp the abiding and perfect covenant of grace was unconditional and did not include the moral law written on the heart at creation and summed up in the ten commandments given to Israel. In short, his position seemed to imperil the perpetuity of the moral law as a rule of life for believers and was antinomian in its tendency. It is further excluded in the Confession 19.5,6.[28]

---

27 Tobias Crisp, *Christ Alone Exalted* [1643], Vol 2, Sermon 2, 247–251. David Dickson, *Truth's Victory over Error* (Glasgow, 1773) sees the closing sentence of WCF 7.6 as reference to Socinian error.

28 See also J.V.Fesko, *Theology*, 155ff.

Appendix – legacy issues

1. Rejection of infant baptism

John Tombes was an Anglican clergyman of Presbyterian views on church government who scrupled infant baptism from the late 1620s. He was a vigorous controversialist. In December 1645, he published *Two treatises and an appendix to them concerning Infant-Baptisme*, part of which he had submitted to the Westminster Assembly, but his position was not supported.

Tombes argued that the covenant with Abraham (Gen. 17) was a mixed covenant of works and grace. He picked up on the 78th proposition advanced by John Cameron in his 1608 three-covenant scheme which stated 'Circumcision, primarily, did separate between the seed of Abraham and the rest of the nations; it did seal unto them the earthly promise: secondarily, it did signify our sanctification.'[29] Apparently also following **Robert Bellarmine** (1542–1621), the capable Roman Catholic apologist, Tombes considered that circumcision sealed only earthly benefits to Abraham's posterity.[30] As baptism sealed spiritual benefits the connection between circumcision and baptism maintained by those baptising infants was broken. The covenant of grace promulgated by Christ was unconditional but both the Abrahamic covenant of Genesis 17 and the Sinai covenant required conditions on the part of those party to them. The natural seed of Abraham inherited temporal benefits and the spiritual seed gospel blessings.

---

29 Samuel Bolton, *True Bounds* (1856 edition), 399–400; also cited by Tombes, Two Treatises, 4.

30 This was claimed by Puritans such as William Ames, Thomas Shepard of New England and John Flavel; see Joel R Beeke and Mark Jones, *A Puritan Theology* (Grand Rapids: Reformation Heritage, 2016), 736.

Subsequent debate saw many of those of congregational church government who opposed infant baptism develop their argument, so that both the Abrahamic covenant and the Sinai covenant were seen as versions of the covenant of works. Nehemiah Coxe (d. 1689), one of the authors of the 1677 London Confession, regards the covenant in Genesis 12 as one of grace being free of conditions, but that in Genesis 17 as one of works, a prelude to the Sinai covenant. In a man like Philip Cary (d. 1710), who engaged in significant debate with John Flavel in 1690, there is a radical distinction. Anything of the nature of promise without conditions attached is seen as a covenant of grace (e.g. Gen. 17:1–9) but anything stating a condition makes it a legal covenant (so Gen. 17:10). However, as Mark Jones rightly states: 'The demand to perform something in a covenant does not make it a covenant of works by default. Rather, divine grace and human responsibility belong together in the covenant of grace.'[31]

2. *John Owen*

The great **John Owen** (1616–83) deals with the subject of the Mosaic covenant in an extended discussion in his massive multi-volume Commentary on Hebrews, particularly at Hebrews 8:6, (included in Volume 3 published in 1680). He indeed acknowledges that the difference between the majority two-covenant view (the covenant of works and a twofold administration of the covenant of grace), and the three-covenant form which he holds is not so much, given the measure of agreement, but he is in a minority category with a few others like Samuel Petto (c. 1624–1711). Owen holds clearly to the covenant of works but the comparison

31 Joel R Beeke and Mark Jones, *A Puritan Theology*, 734.

and contrast of the two covenants, the old covenant of Moses, and the new covenant of Christ (2 Cor. 3:6–9; Gal. 4:24–26; Heb. 7:22; 9:15–20) is such as to suggest to him that these are two quite different covenants. Hence, he could be classed as holding a form of three-covenant view such as was advanced by John Cameron in 1608, although he does not use Cameron's 'subservient' terminology but speaks of the Sinai covenant being 'superadded'. In fact, he cannot be neatly classified because of his own nuances.

For Owen, the Mosaic covenant was not a dispensation of the covenant of grace properly speaking but a particular temporary covenant 'revealing for certain ends, the notion, sense and power of the first covenant [of works] and preparative of the full revelation and declaration of the latter [covenant of grace] by Jesus Christ, who was in all things to have the pre-eminence, as that it is not easy to discern and distinguish what belongs unto the one in them and what to the other, or from whether of them they are to be denominated.'[32]

It was not a revived covenant of works for sinful men, for they already stood under its curse, but it did declare the moral content of the covenant of works. No saving benefit was secured by the Mosaic covenant as such, but believers were saved during its existence through the abiding Abrahamic promissary covenant fulfilled in Christ which operated throughout. The Sinai covenant was rather to be seen as declaring the legal condition for Christ under the new covenant and in that sense was a covenant of works for him.

32 John Owen's introductory commendation of Samuel Petto, *The Difference Between the Old and New Covenant Stated and Explained* (London, 1674). Samuel D. Renihan, *From Shadow to Substance: The Federal Theology of the English Particular Baptists 1642–1704* (Oxford: Centre for Baptist History and Heritage, 2018) provides detailed discussion of the development of Particular Baptist Covenant Theology.

Complicating the complexity in understanding his position, Owen considers that the covenant of grace, viewed as the successive promises of grace before Christ, is not strictly a covenant until Christ established it by his death. It then became a 'testament' that is, it possessed the formal nature of a covenant. The Sinai covenant is also a testament because it involved sacrifice. For Owen it was important to contrast the old and new covenants to highlight the greater revelation of grace in the new and the particular privileges of worship that can now be enjoyed.

3. Puritan confessions compared

It is of interest to compare the Puritan creeds on the covenant of grace (Table 7). It has to be realised that the covenants of works and covenant of grace are theological terms seeking to reflect biblical teaching and they need to be distinguished from the biblical terms for Moses (the old covenant) and Christ (the new covenant). Westminster sets out the classic two covenant scheme. Savoy, the Confession of the Congregational-Independents to which Owen had significant input, omits detailed description of the ways in which the covenant of grace was administered under Moses and under the gospel and in effect is more inclusive of different views on how to understand it.

The London Confession of 1677/89 of Calvinistic Baptists refers to the covenant of grace in 7.2, but in 7.3 it departs from the other Confessions in speaking of the covenant of grace in terms of promises that are steps towards the full realisation of the new covenant. On the surface there may seem no issue, but the wording does allow for views such as those already noted of

Nehemiah Coxe, an author of the London Confession, and other Particular Baptists who, unlike Owen, considered the covenants in the Old Testament as preparatory, in that they provided no warrant for the continuation of the administration of the covenant on the household principle. The circumcision of children in the Old Testament was regarded as belonging to earthly privileges and providing no justification for the admission of infants into the spiritual privilege of church membership by baptism.

The covenant of grace was equated with the transaction accomplished by Christ and the fullness of the new covenant promise of a regenerate people who know their God and are indwelt by the Spirit. On this basis, the church on earth must have a professedly regenerate membership and not be coextensive with the community as some then common forms of the Church-State relations held. Clearly there were real biblical concerns about the nature of the church on earth by those of congregational polity, even though Owen and Savoy were in agreement with Westminster on the baptism of the infant children of professing believers.

The London Confession also bases the new covenant on what is known in theology as the covenant of redemption. Savoy does this too by an insertion in Chapter 8:1 shown in italics thus: 'It pleased God, in his eternal purpose, to choose and ordain the Lord Jesus, his only begotten Son, according to a covenant made between them both, to be the Mediator....' Westminster is not at all opposed to the covenant of redemption but, as noted on page 79, this position gained more general standing after 1647, and indeed is clearer in the Larger Catechism. which traces the covenant back to the eternal purpose in Christ.[33]

33 Note also J.V. Fesko, *Theology*, 163–66.

TABLE 7

WESTMINSTER, 1646	SAVOY, 1658	BAPTIST, 1677/89
7.5: This covenant was differently administered in the time of the law, and in the time of the Gospel: under the law it was administered by promises, prophecies, sacrifices, circumcision, the paschal lamb, and other types and ordinances delivered to the people of the Jews, all fore-signifying Christ to come; which were, for that time, sufficient and efficacious, through the operation of the Spirit, to instruct and build up the elect in faith in the promised Messiah, by whom they had full remission of sins, and eternal salvation; and is called the old Testament. **7.6:** Under the Gospel, when Christ, the substance, was exhibited, the ordinances in which this covenant is dispensed are the preaching of the Word, and the administration of the sacraments of Baptism and the Lord's Supper: which, though fewer in number, and administered with more simplicity, and less outward glory, yet, in them, it is held forth in more fullness, evidence, and spiritual efficacy, to all nations, both Jews and Gentiles; and is called the new Testament. There are not therefore two covenants of grace, differing in substance, but one and the same, under various dispensations.	**7.5:** Although this covenant hath been differently and variously administered in respect of ordinances and institutions in the time of the law, and since the coming of Christ in the flesh; yet for the substance and efficacy of it, to all its spiritual and saving ends, it is one and the same; upon the account of which various dispensations, it is called the Old and New Testament. **Omits 7.6**	**7.3:** This covenant is revealed in the gospel; first of all to Adam in the promise of salvation by the seed of the woman, and afterwards by farther steps, until the full discovery thereof was completed in the New Testament; and it is founded in the eternal covenant transaction that was between the Father and the Son about the redemption of the elect; and it is alone by the grace of this covenant that all of the posterity of fallen Adam that ever were saved did obtain life and blessed immortality, man now being utterly incapable of acceptance with God upon those terms on which Adam stood in his state of innocency. **Omits 7.4, 5, & 6**

19

IS THE ADAMIC COVENANT SET ASIDE?

By the law of creation and by the covenant of works humanity was bound to obedience both positively and negatively under threat of punishment. By his disobedience Adam had been brought under the curse of that covenant. He and all those he represented became children of wrath, with the fullness of the sanctions of the covenant in eternal punishment upon them. Adam could no longer attain life by obedience.

However, God's commitment to his creation continued in the face of human sin. God immediately announces the promise of forgiveness and eternal life through the Seed of the Woman (Gen. 3:15) The promised enmity between the woman's seed and the seed of the serpent in subsequent history is evident and comes to a climax in Christ's defeat of the Devil and his works. On the basis of the covenant of redemption within the Trinity, Jesus will be obedient to the covenant of works in the believers' place, and his righteousness as the one justified before God will be reckoned to his people, and the renewing and indwelling Spirit granted them. However, the covenant of works, being based on man's nature and the moral law written on his heart, continues to be the rule of life for believers in so far as the moral law is incorporated in it.

God's claim to obedience is not ended by humanity's rebellion. Unbelievers continue to be subject to the covenant of works as a duty and obligation although it can no longer justify them. Further, the conditional promise remains in effect although it cannot be met (Lev. 18:5; Matt. 19:17; Rom. 10:5; Gal. 3:12).[1]

As noted, the covenant of works involved the moral law of love for God and neighbour that was written on Adam's heart at his creation. That law is expressed briefly in the ten commandments in a manner appropriate to the time and circumstances of Israel. The Mosaic covenant is superseded in Christ, but the ten commandments, received from the hand of Christ rather than from Moses, remain as the rule of life for believers.[2] They have been justified by faith in Christ in order that the righteousness of the law might be fulfilled in them as they walk in the new way of the Spirit (Rom. 8:4).

The Moral Law, the Covenant of Works and the Decalogue

Wollebius (1626): 'The divine law transmitted by Moses, differs in form, not in content, from the natural law given to the first man, vestiges of which can also be found among the gentiles. (Rom. 2:14–15: "The gentiles, who have not the law, do by nature what the law requires; they are a law to themselves. They show that the law is written on their hearts.")'[3]

Burgess (1647): 'And when we say, the Law was before Moses, I do not mean only that it was written in the hearts of men, but

1 A good summary appears in L. Berkhof, *Systematic Theology* (London: Banner of Truth, 1958), 218.

2 The unitary nature of the Mosaic law and yet the legitimacy of recognising the special place of the ten commandments is discussed on page 232.

3 J. Wollebius, *Reformed Dogmatics*, 75.

it was publicly preached in the ministry that the Church did then enjoy, as appears by Noah's preaching...So that we may say, the Decalogue is Adam's and Abraham's, and Noah's, and Christ's, and the Apostles, as well as Moses'.[4]

The Abrogation of the Covenant of Works

Witsius (1677) enumerates the law, the promise and the threatening in the covenant as abiding: 'And first, we are very certain that there are many things in this covenant of immutable and eternal truth, which we reckon up in this order: (1) the precepts of the covenant, excepting that probationary one, oblige all, and every one to a perfect performance of duty, in what state soever they are. (2) Eternal life, promised by the covenant, can be obtained upon no other condition, than that of perfect, and in every respect complete obedience. (3) No act of disobedience escapes the vengeance of God, and death is always the punishment for sin.'[5]

On the other hand, there are changes. It is no longer possible to obtain life by our obedience, although it is possible for a suitable Surety to bear the curse due to us for sin and to render obedience in our stead, so gaining for us both forgiveness and eternal life.

The Moral Law as the Rule of Life for the Believer

Rollock (1597): 'I confess good works be required of them which be in Christ, and justified by him: but all such works belong to grace and regeneration; to grace, I say, only; and they be not the works of free will or of nature. Know this then, that to such as be

4 Anthony Burgess, *Vindiciae Legis*, 150.
5 Hermann Witsius, *Economy*, I.ix, 151

in Christ, the covenant of works to them is abolished, and of none effect so far forth as by it justification and salvation is obtained. I grant, the law abides which is a rule of those works, which properly and specially did first appertain to the covenant of works: but now it hath another special use; for it serves as our direction in the works of grace and sanctification. So then the law has ceased, as it was the rule of the works of nature required in the covenant of grace: but it is still in use to them which are in Christ, as it the rule of the works of grace.'[6]

Faith and Works in Justification

The Irish Articles (1615) #36 recount a typical presentation of the believer's works in relation to justification which it may be appropriate to note here:

> 'When we say that we are justified by faith only, we do not mean that the said justifying faith is alone in man, without true Repentance, Hope, Charity, and the fear of God (for such a faith is dead, and cannot justify), neither do we mean that this our act to believe in Christ, nor this our faith in Christ, which is within us, doth of itself justify us, nor deserve our justification unto us (for that were to account ourselves to be justified by the virtue or dignity of some thing that is within ourselves):
>
> but the true understanding and meaning thereof is that although we have Faith, Hope, Charity, Repentance, and the fear of God within us and add never so many good works thereunto: yet we must renounce the merit of all our said virtues, of Faith, Hope, Charity, and all our other virtues, and good deeds, which we either

6 Robert Rollock, *A Treatise of God's Effectual Calling*, 10.

have done, shall do, or can do, as things that be far too weak and imperfect, and insufficient to deserve remission of our sins, and our justification: and therefore we must trust only in God's mercy, and the merits of his most dearly beloved Son, our only Redeemer, Saviour, and Justifier, Jesus Christ.

Nevertheless, because Faith doth directly send us to Christ for our justification, and that by faith given us of God we embrace the promise of God's mercy, and the remission of our sin (which thing none other of our virtues or works properly doth): therefore the Scripture saith, that Faith without works; and the ancient fathers of the Church to the same purpose, that only Faith doth justify us.'

20

SIGNIFICANCE OF COVENANT THEOLOGY

For convenience the following brief summary of the significance of the covenant for theology is provided.

The Covenant Expresses the High Point of True Religion

God is greatly exalted above his creatures but the covenant is the expression of an intimate bond of love not otherwise possible. It is God's plan and purpose. Emphasis on the stipulations by God and the obligations on humanity must not lead us to caricature the covenant as a mere commercial contract. This would be a gross distortion. God is love, and his covenant with Adam reflects that. It is a covenant between friends and lovers, the means by which those not equals may pledge mutual fidelity.

John Barret (1675): 'Men that covenant with one another aim at their own advantage; but God, in Covenanting with his Creatures, doth not expect any benefit, or advantage by them, but does it to show how willing and ready he is to communicate his blessings to them.'[1]

1 John Barret, *Good will toward men* (London, 1675), 44.

The Covenant Opens the Way to a Bright Future

God and humanity are on a journey and through God's goodness the covenant means humanity's full potential can be realised and the goal reached. There was a certain ambivalence about the life promised in early covenant thinking but greater clarity is in time achieved. God aims not only to provide a blessing and reward to which humanity could not otherwise attain, but to crown humanity with glory and honour in his presence for ever.

Samuel Rutherford (1655): 'Communion with God in glory, is a reward not due by nature, but by the free gift of God to the most perfect law obedience...But that Adam should have such an eminent life for the reward of his obedience as communion with God, which is far above his obedience, is the free donation of God...'[2]

The Covenant Assures to us Consistency in God's Relationship with His Creatures

God's covenant relationship with creation and particularly with humanity assures us of a predictable world and a consistency in God's relationship with it. If there was no covenant relationship, consideration of the power of God as the Creator and his authority as Governor of all things might suggest a very insecure position for us. God deals with us by covenant to bind us closer to him in love.

Burgess (1646): 'Consider why God will deal with man in a covenant way rather than in a mere absolute supreme way. There may be these reasons: (1) That God might sweeten and endear

2 Samuel Rutherford, *The Covenant of Life Opened*, 22.

himself to us ... for God did not make man because he needed him but that there might be objects to whom he would communicate his love. (2) Another reason might be to incite and encourage Adam the more to obedience...to do a duty because of a reward offered is not a slavish and unlawful thing... (3) That thereby Adam's obedience might be more willing and free. An absolute law might seem to extort obedience, but a covenant and agreement makes it to appear more free and willing...'[3]

The Covenant Accounts for the Ethical Unity of Humanity

The covenant more adequately accounts for the spread of sin to Adam's descendants than natural transmission, for it operates on the principle of representative or federal headship and imputation, as is also the case with Christ and believers. 'For just as by one man's disobedience the many were made sinners, so also by the obedience of one man the many will be made righteous' (Rom. 5:19).

Bucanus (1605): 'Moreover, that which Christ hath done as head of the Church and of all the elect, is imputed to the Church, and we are said in Christ to have kept the law, to have been dead, buried and raised again, and to sit in the heavens, Ephesians 2:6 and many other places. Therefore Adam's sin, as head of mankind, is rightly imputed to us, because whatever was done by him was supposed to be done by all men and every individual man, and he represented his whole flock. Therefore also did he lose that which was committed to his keeping for his whole flock.'[4]

---

3 Anthony Burgess, *Vindiciae legis* (London, 1647), 127–128.
4 William Bucanus, *Institutions* (London, 1606), 162.

A covenant framework also ensures that one is focused on the progressive historical unfolding of God's purposes, and should be a valuable corrective to any tendency to impose dogmatic conclusions on the text of Scripture. Cocceius was well aware of this, and the weaknesses in his expression of it should not mean that we do not draw the conclusion.

PART FOUR

Covenant Theology, 1701–2000

21

THE COVENANT OF WORKS IN THE BRITISH ISLES

If one omits the discussions on the various national religious covenants in Scotland, there was little in the way of development of Covenant Theology in the 18th century. Those who trained for the Scottish Presbyterian ministry in the 18th century did not usually have large libraries, nor were the texts in theology locally sourced. The professor would utilise a Latin text by an established European theologian. The writings of men such as **Benedict Pictet** (1675–1724), son-in-law of Francis Turretin and professor at Geneva from 1686, and **Johann Van Marck** (1655–1731) of Leiden, were popular.[1] Turretin was used in the Secession Church in the 1740s by Ebenezer Erskine.[2]

1 See Jack C. Whytock, *'An Educated Clergy' Scottish Theological Education and Training in the Kirk and the Secession, 1560–1859* (Oregon: Wipf & Stock, 2007). Pictet's *Theologica Christiana* (1696) was translated into English as late as 1834: *Christian Theology* translated from the Latin by Frederick Reyroux (London: R. B. Seeley and W. Burnside, 1834).

2 J.R.Beeke and Randall J.Pederson in introduction to John Brown, *The Systematic Theology of John Brown of Haddington* (Fearn: Christian Focus, 2002), i. An edition of Turretin's 3 volume work in Latin was printed in Edinburgh in 1847.

The Marrow Theology

As a result of a recommendation by **Thomas Boston** (1676–1732) of the book to a friend, James Hog published a new edition of Edward Fisher's *The Marrow of Modern Divinity* in 1718. Over against the legalistic strain of teaching called neonomianism, which had affected the church, the *Marrow* was calculated to help present the gospel to sinners in a way which magnified the grace of God. However, its unusual expressions, rendered all the less clear by the lack of familiarity with earlier editions of the book and the writings on which it was based,[3] contributed to the famous Marrow Controversy (1718–1723) in the Church of Scotland during which the book was condemned by the Church's General Assembly. Boston himself issued an edition of the *Marrow* with notes in 1726 which has been often reprinted. His extremely popular *Human Nature in its Fourfold State* (Edinburgh 1720, and reprinted perhaps 100 times since), as well as his posthumous work *A View of the Covenant of Works from the Sacred Records* (Edinburgh 1772), maintain the common early position. He regarded the covenant of grace as made with Christ as head of the elect and did not posit a distinct covenant of redemption of the Father with the Son as the foundation of the covenant of grace.

The same feature is found in the work of **John Brown** of Haddington (1722–87) who was appointed Professor by the Associate Synod (Burgher) in 1768. His lectures on theology entitled *A Compendious View of Natural and Revealed Religion* were

3 It was printed seven times in London to 1650, and another two times there to 1699. Hog reprinted the 1699 edition in Edinburgh. The book drew from the writings of numerous Reformed authors prior to 1646, and was written in a context of antinomian influence with a view to countering the same. D. C. Lachman, *The Marrow Controversy* (Edinburgh: Rutherford House, 1988) is a standard study; see also Willian Vandoodewaard, *The Marrow Controversy and Seceder Tradition.*

issued in 1782.[4] **John Colquhoun** (1748–1827), another Marrow supporter, issued his *Treatise on the Covenant of Works* in Edinburgh in 1821.

James Fisher (1697–1775) was a founder of the Secession Church along with the Erskines. He succeeded Ebenezer Erskine as theological tutor 1749–64. Here follows the relevant section of his *The Assembly's Shorter Catechism Explained*, in its 1765 edition.

JAMES FISHER'S CATECHISM

Q. 1. Was there any thing special in God's government of man, when he was created, above the other creatures?

A. Yes; for God gave man a moral law, which the other creatures, not endued with reason, were not capable of: Job 35:10, 11—"None saith, Where is God my maker?—Who teacheth us more than the beasts of the earth, and maketh us wiser than the fowls of heaven."

Q. 2. What call you a moral law?

A. A moral law signifies a law of right manners, or good and suitable behaviour towards God and man, and adapted to man's rational nature, Rom. 7:12.

Q. 3. How was this law first given to man?

A. It was written upon the table of his heart, the moment that God created him in his own image, Gen. 1:27.

4 Reprinted several times, most recently under the title in the footnote #2 above.

Q. 4. What do you understand by God's writing the law upon the table of his heart?

A. God's inlaying a principle of obedience in his heart, disposing him to obey out of love to God, and a supreme regard to his authority, Eccl. 7:29.

Q. 5. What was the peculiar favour which God manifested to man in a state of innocence, besides writing the law upon his heart?

A. The reducing that law to the form of a covenant, by which man became confederate with heaven.

Q. 6. What is a covenant?

A. A mutual free compact and agreement between two parties, upon express terms or conditions.

Q. 7. How many covenants are there, relating to the life and happiness of man?

A. Two; the covenant of works, and the covenant of grace, Gal. 4:24 - "These are the two covenants."

Q. 8. Which of these was the covenant which God entered into with man, when he was created?

A. The covenant of works, or of life.

Q. 9. Why called a covenant of works?

A. From the condition of it.

Q. 10. Why called a covenant of life?

A. From the promise of it.

Q. 11. How does it appear that God entered into a covenant with man in innocence?

A. From the condition and penalty that were in the first covenant, Gen. 2:16, 17, and from express mention in Scripture of Adam's breach of that covenant. Hos. 6:7—"But they, like men, (margin, like Adam,) have transgressed the covenant."

Q. 12. How does it appear that Adam gave that consent, which was necessary in a mutual covenant?

A. His silent acquiescence to the will of his sovereign Creator, implied a consent; and his consent could not be withheld, by a creature made after the image of God, in knowledge, righteousness, and holiness.

Q. 13. What was the condition of the covenant of works?

A. Perfect obedience to the whole law of God, in heart and life.

Q. 14. What was the sum of that law, which was the rule of man's covenant obedience?

A. That man believe whatever God shall reveal, and do whatever he shall command, Rom. 10:5; and, in testimony of it, not to eat of the tree of knowledge of good and evil, Gen. 2:17.

Q. 15. Was this prohibition, of not eating of the tree of knowledge of good and evil, a moral or a positive precept?

A. It was a positive precept, founded in the sovereign will of God.

Q. 16. Was it then a thing in itself indifferent to eat, or not to eat, of that tree?

A. There could be no moral evil in eating of that tree, more than any other, antecedently to the command of God forbidding it; but after that, it was no more indifferent, but highly sinful to do so.

Q. 17. Why did God extend the rule and matter of man's covenant obedience, to a thing in itself indifferent?

A. That man's obedience might turn upon the precise point of the will of God, which is the plainest evidence of true obedience, Psalm 40:8.

Q. 18. Did man's life and death hang upon this positive precept about the forbidden fruit?

A. Not upon this only, but likewise on the whole law, Gal. 3:10. "Cursed is every one that continueth not in all things written in the book of the law to do them."

Q. 19. Was there any mercy or favour in restricting man from eating of this tree?

A. Much every way; for this restriction taught him, that though he was lord of the creatures, yet he was God's subject: it was a beacon set up before him to beware of sin; and it pointed him away from the creatures to God himself for happiness.

Q. 20. What was the penalty in case of disobedience?

A. It was the pain of death:—"In the day that thou eatest thereof thou shalt surely die," Gen. 2:17.

Q. 21. What kind of death was this which was threatened upon disobedience?

A. It was death temporal, spiritual, and eternal.

Q. 22. Did Adam die a temporal or natural death, that day he sinned?

A. No; but he became a dead man in law, and his body got its death-wound, and became mortal, Rom. 5:12.

Q. 23. Why was the immediate execution of natural death suspended?

A. Because of his posterity then in his loins; and because of another covenant that was prepared, Job 33:24.

Q. 24. What was the spiritual death threatened?

A. The loss of his original righteousness, and the favour of God, Gen. 3:8, 10, 24.

Q. 25. What is meant by eternal death?

A. The enduring of the wrath of God, in soul and body, in a state of separation from him for ever, Matt. 25:46.

Q. 26. What was the promise in this covenant, in case of obedience?

A. It was life.

Q. 27. How does it appear that life was promised, when the promise of it is not expressly mentioned?

A. The promise of life is included in the threatening of death; "In the day that thou eatest thereof, thou shalt surely die:" which necessarily implies, If thou dost not eat thereof, thou shalt surely live, Gal. 3:12.

Q. 28. What kind of life was it that was promised to man in the covenant of works?

A. The continuance of his natural life, consisting in the union of his soul and body; the continuance also of his spiritual life, consisting in the favour of God, Lev. 18:5; and his entering upon eternal life in heaven, after he had passed through the time of his trial upon earth, Rom. 7:10.

Q. 29. How do you prove that eternal life in heaven was included in the promise of this covenant?

A. From eternal death in hell being included in the threatening of it, as the natural wages of sin; and from Christ himself expounding the promise of the covenant of works of eternal life, Matt. 19:16. When one puts the question to him, "What shall I do, that I may inherit eternal life?" he answers, ver. 17—"If thou wilt enter into life, (namely, eternal life, by doing,) keep the commandments."

Q. 30. Was there any proportion between Adam's obedience, though sinless, and the life that was promised?

A. There can be no proportion between the obedience of a finite creature, however perfect, and the enjoyment of the infinite God, Job 22:2, 3—"Can a man be profitable to God? Is it any pleasure to the Almighty, that thou art righteous? or, is it gain to him, that thou makest thy way perfect?"

Q. 31. Why could not Adam's perfect obedience be meritorious of eternal life?

A. Because perfect obedience was no more than what he was bound to, by virtue of his natural dependence on God, as a reasonable creature made after his image.

Q. 32. Could he have claimed the reward as a debt, in case he had continued in his obedience?

A. He could have claimed it only as a pactional [agreed] debt, in virtue of the covenant promise, by which God became debtor to his own faithfulness, but not in virtue of any intrinsic merit of his obedience, Luke 17:10.

Q. 33. What then was the grace and condescension of God that shined in the covenant of works?

A. In that he entered into a covenant, at all, with his own creature; and promised eternal life as a reward of his work, though he had nothing to work with, but what he received from God, 1 Cor. 4:7.

Q. 34. Did the covenant of works oblige man to seek life upon the account of his obedience?

A. It left man to expect it upon his obedience, but did not oblige him to seek it on that score; but only on account of the faithfulness of God in his promise, graciously annexing life to man's sinless obedience, Matt. 19:16.

Q. 35. Did the covenant of works oblige man to make his own life and happiness the chief end of his obedience?

A. By no means: the promise of life was an encouragement to his obedience, but the glory of God was to be the chief end in it; to which any view of his own happiness was to be subordinate, otherwise his obedience had not been perfect.

Q. 36. Was the covenant of works a law, as well as a covenant?

A. Yes; it was both the one and the other.

Q. 37. In what respect was it a law?

A. As it was not between equals, but enjoined by the sovereign Lawgiver.

Q. 38. In what respect was it a covenant?

A. As it contained a promise of reward, graciously annexed to the precept, Gal. 3:12.

Q. 39. Is this covenant abrogated, or still in force?

A. It was never abrogated, but is still binding upon all that are under it, Matt. 5:18, and 19:17.

Q. 40. Did not man's sin abrogate this covenant?

A. No; his sin bound him under the curse of it, Gal. 3:10.

Q. 41. Did not Christ's doing and dying abrogate this covenant of works?

A. No; it fulfilled both the precept and penalty of it, Rom. 10:4.

Q. 42. Does not the law of faith abrogate the law of works?

A. No; "Do we make void the law through faith? God forbid; yea, we establish the law," Rom. 3:31.

Q. 43. Are sinners, that live under the gospel dispensation, under the same obligation to obedience, as the condition of life, that Adam was under?

A. While they remain in unbelief, rejecting the surety of the better testament, they keep themselves under an obligation to do the whole law, and so are under the curse of it, Gal. 5:3, 4.

Q. 44. What may we learn from this doctrine?

A. It teaches us, that eternal death comes by the breach of the covenant of works in the first Adam; and that eternal life comes only by the fulfilling of the same covenant by the second Adam, Rom. 5:19.

The Economy of the Covenants by Herman Witsius became available in English translation in 1769, and was often reprinted. **George Hill** became Professor in St Mary's College at St Andrews in 1780. His *Theological Institutes* was published in 1803, and in expanded form in 1821. This was a standard work in Scotland for many years.[5] It is orthodox enough, but its treatment of the covenant of works is limited to a page or two.

Marrow influence, as well as that of the Thirty-nine Articles and the Westminster Confession can be seen in the little-known Welsh Calvinistic Confession of 1823.[6]

The method of gospel presentation in terms of the covenants of works and grace was usual in the British Isles until the middle of the 19th century among the Calvinistic churches. Thereafter it suffered decline as the robust Reformed theology was diluted to a more general evangelicalism. Fisher's catechism is as good a summary as one could find of the common position of those of Reformed persuasion.

The Scottish Congregationalist preacher, **David Russell** (1779–1848), wrote on the Adamic dispensation and also on the Old and New Covenants in 1824, but there is nothing startling in his work. T. & T. Clark in Edinburgh published George Steward's *Mediatorial Sovereignty, the Mystery of Christ and the Revelation of the Old and New Testaments* in 1863. It seeks to grapple with issues of Adam's relation to God, generally in line with the traditional theology but in a somewhat fresh way.

---

5 5th edition 1850; 6th edition 1854.

6 Published for the General Assembly by D. O'Brien Owen at Caernarvon, 1900, pp. 50–51. I am indebted to Revd. Richard Holst of Hull and Revd. Gwyn Davies for access to a copy of this Confession and for information about it given in January 2002. *The Marrow of Modern Divinity* was published in Welsh as early as 1651. The Welsh Confession was effectively dispensed with in 1924 with the publication and adoption of *A Short Declaration of Faith and Practice*. It was more formally consigned to the archive in 1933 when the Presbyterian Church of Wales adopted Declaratory Articles as part of a re-constitution under Act of Parliament.

TABLE 8

WELSH CALVINISTIC METHODIST CONFESSION, 1823

9. OF THE COVENANT OF WORKS

It pleased God to condescend to enter into covenant with the first man, Adam, adapted to his state of innocence, and consisting of a command, a threat, and a promise. The special command, which was the pledge of his obedience, was not to eat the fruit of the forbidden tree; the threat was that, if he ate thereof, he should die. The nature of the command and the threat leads us to infer that this covenant contained a promise also of life and happiness, if man obeyed the command, in contradistinction to the death threatened as the penalty of disobedience. [Gen. 2:16,17; Hos. 6:7; Rom. 5:12–21; Rom. 7:10; Rom. 10:5 etc; 1 Cor. 15:22, 43–49; Matt. 19:17] The law of our nature was all contained in this covenant, so that it was impossible to transgress the special command of the covenant without transgressing, at the same time, the entire law of our nature. [James 2:10] Adam stood, in this covenant, not only as a natural root of all his offspring, but also as their covenant head and representative; so that their happiness or misery, as well as his own, depended upon his obedience or disobedience. [Gen. 2; Gen. 3; 1 Cor. 15:22; Rom. 5:12,18,19]

10. OF THE FALL OF MAN, AND ORIGINAL SIN

Though man, when God made the covenant of works with him, had power to obey and fulfil the conditions of the covenant, yet he disobeyed God and broke the covenant. [Eccl. 7:29; Rom. 5:12,18–19] The serpent deceived Eve, and Adam hearkened unto the voice of his wife and wilfully transgressed the command of his Creator by eating of the forbidden fruit; and by this means he broke God's covenant [Gen. 3:6–8,13; 2 Cor. 11:3; Rom. 3:23], forfeited his right to the promised life, became subject to the threatened death [Rom 5:12; Gal. 3:10; Eph. 2:1; Ti. 3:3; Jer. 17:9], lost his original righteousness and fellowship with God, and became totally corrupt in soul and body [Eccl. 7:29; Psalm 14:1–4; Rom. 3:10–19; Rom. 8:7–8; Job 14:4; Mark 7:21–23; Ti. 1:15; Col. 1:21] As he was the root and representative of mankind, his first sin is imputed to them, and his corruption flows into all his seed, who spring from him by natural generation. [Rom. 5:12–21; 1 Cor. 15:21–22]

11. OF THE STATE OF MAN BY NATURE

All mankind are by nature in a guilty, sinful, and miserable state [Isa. 64:6; Eph. 2:3; Psalm 51:5]. By their relation to the first Adam they are under the law, as it is sanctioned in the covenant of works: and through his first transgression, all of them, forasmuch as they are in him, have been brought under the curse of the law [Rom. 5:12, 18; 1 Cor. 15:22; Deut. 27:26; Gal. 3:10], which declares everyone cursed that continues not in all things which are written in the book of the law to do them.

Hugh Martin (1822–85), a minister of the Free Church of Scotland, made good use of Covenant Theology in his book *The Atonement* (London, 1870). **John Laidlaw**'s valuable Cunningham Lectures, *The Bible Doctrine of Man* (1879), sufficiently indicate the author's belief in the covenant of works without discussing it as a topic. Cautioning against the view that redemption is merely the recovery of what was lost by the fall, he writes: 'Scripture conveys not obscurely the idea that the type of redeemed man is higher than that of man unfallen; that the second creation when completed, shall excel what the first had been even had it remained unsullied by sin; that as we have borne the image of the earthly, so shall we bear the image of the heavenly; and that when earth and heavens are dissolved, "we look for a new heavens and a new earth wherein dwells righteousness."'[7]

7 John Laidlaw, *The Bible Doctrine of Man* (Edinburgh: T & T Clark, 1879), 135.

22

THE COVENANT OF WORKS IN THE NETHERLANDS

The situation with Covenant Theology in the Dutch churches is one where there is considerable neglect for about 100 years until the later part of the 19th century. The neo-Calvinistic movement associated with Abraham Kuyper and Herman Bavinck (1854–1921) corresponds with a resurgence of interest, so that Bavinck provides one of the finest overall statements of the covenant of works and its significance known to the present writer.[1]

There was one important historical incident in 1748 and later involving the views of Rev. Antonious van der Os the newly installed young rationalistic minister of Zwolle. Among his errors was rejection of the federal headship of Adam, while in 1752 he preached a sermon in which he rejected the idea of binding Confessions of Faith. This led to the first discipline case in the Dutch churches involving doctrine since the Synod of Dordt, despite Prince William IV and some of the Professors at Leiden being themselves affected by rationalism. The Scots-born minister of Woubrugge, some miles from Leiden, Dr **Alexander**

1 Bavinck's *Gereformeerde Dogmatiek* has been published in English translation in four volumes as *Reformed Dogmatics* (Grand Rapids: Baker, 2003–2008). For the covenant of works see especially Vol 2, 563ff; in the abridged one volume edition of 2011, 329ff.

Comrie (1708–74), took a major part in resisting the rationalistic influences, and had grass-roots support. He and his friend and fellow author, **Nicolaus Holtius**, issued an anonymous series of tracts between 1753–59 entitled *Examen van het Ontwerp van Tolerantie* [Examination of the Concept of Tolerance]. They were strictly Reformed in a manner typical of the 17th century. The *Examen* was supressed by the authorities in 1761. Two professors of Leiden, John Van den Honert and J. J. Schultens, disputed with Comrie and Holtius. Although the Leiden professors were not out and out defenders of Van der Os, they held that Comrie and Holtius read things into the confessions in order to bind ministers to these opinions. The covenant of works, which is not explicit in the Dutch confessions, was one matter in view. Comrie was one of the last defenders of traditional Calvinism in the Dutch churches of the time, and was a very important figure. Probably converted through Ebenezer Erskine, he was a supporter of the Marrow theology and translated some of Boston's work.[2]

In the work of **J.J. Van Oosterzee** (1817–82), Professor in the University of Utrecht, one sees a presentation that rejects a pre-fall covenant as of not the slightest dogmatic importance: 'Scripture does not teach that God has made a contract with man, but only that he designs to lead him, plainly by a moral road, to greater happiness.'[3]

2 There is not much on Comrie in English. A brief survey based on A. Kuyper is Geoffrey Thomas, 'Alexander Comrie' in *Banner of Truth Magazine* #65–66 (Feb–Mar 1969); an important reference is J.R.Beeke, *Assurance of Faith* (New York: Peter Lang, 1994), 280ff.

3 J.J.Van Oosterzee, *Christian Dogmatics* (London: Hodder & Stoughton, 1878), 381. Van Oosterzee was a moderate conservative.

Herman Bavinck

The theology of **Herman Bavinck** reveals a mind well equipped through breadth of study and reflection. Bavinck deliberately chose to study with the University of Leiden's theological faculty, despite its liberal orientation being alien to his own background and beliefs. Shortly afterwards, in 1881, Bavinck edited the 6th and final edition of the *Synopsis purioris theologiae*. This was the famous manual of orthodox Reformed theology first issued in Leiden in 1625.

In Bavinck's *Gereformeerde Dogmatiek* [Reformed Dogmatics], which began to be issued in 1895, one finds a magisterial grasp of the biblical materials and of the theological reflection on them over the centuries of the Christian era. Bavinck stresses that Adam did not possess the highest humanity, a truth implicit in the probationary command, the freedom of choice, and the possibility of sin and death. Adam stood at the beginning and not the end of his career, so that he had to pass on to higher glory or to sin and death. He holds the doctrine of the covenant of works is materially if not formally found in the Belgic Confession Art. 14 and 15 and in Heidelberg Catechism, Lord's Days 3 and 4, and the Canons of Dort III/IV.

While acknowledging that in some hands it was treated in an overly detailed and scholastic manner, Bavinck insists that the covenant of works is based on Scripture and eminently valuable. 'Love, friendship, marriage, as well as all social cooperation in business, industry, science, art, and so forth, is ultimately grounded in a covenant, that is, in reciprocal fidelity and an assortment of generally recognised moral obligations. It should not surprise us, therefore, that also the highest and most richly textured life of human beings, namely, religion, bears this character.' He is not concerned that the word covenant is absent from Genesis 1–2. 'Reformed scholars were never so narrow as to insist on the word, if only the matter itself was certain: one may doubt the word provided the matter is safe.' Bavinck's position is summarised as follows, largely in his own words.[4]

Bavinck insists that without covenant, no religion in the sense of fellowship with God, is possible, since (1) apart from covenant God is either deistically elevated endlessly above the creature, or else pantheistically brought down to the level of the creature. True fellowship can exist only because God is both infinitely great and condescendingly good. (2) The creature has no rights before God since it cannot boast of anything. In his goodness God gives rights to his creature, all gifts of grace, undeserved, unmerited. True religion cannot be anything else than a covenant, since before and after the fall it has its origin in the condescending goodness and grace of God. The covenant of works and the covenant of grace do not differ in their final goal but only in the way that leads to it. (3) God created humans as rational and moral creatures, and he deals with them as such. He wants them to be free and to serve him in love, freely and willingly. Thus religion must take the form of covenant in which love is not coerced, but humans serve God willingly, moved by love to love in return. There is never any right to reward, but it is always grace for us to be allowed to serve God. His the gift, ours the gratitude. Hence true religion is conceivable only in the form of a covenant. The fragmentary statement of the doctrine is immaterial; the matter itself is certain.

4 Herman Bavinck, *Reformed Dogmatics*, 563ff.

The covenant of works includes a further beautiful idea: it gives expression to the fact that humanity before the fall, while having the image of God as a natural endowment (and not a supernatural one as conceived by the Roman Catholics), did not yet possess the highest possible blessing. Adam was not Christ. The natural was not the spiritual. Man lived in the state of one who was changeably good, not the state to which Christ brings us of being unchangeably good, unable to sin, unable to die, above all fear and dread, above all possibility of falling. The recognition that man did not yet have this high state of blessedness also enabled the Reformed generally to avoid exaggerated and idealistic views of the original state in Paradise more common to the Lutherans, who equated salvation with forgiveness. Sin has cosmic significance and has spoiled creation, yet not changed its essence, and the creation ordinances remain in effect. The form of creation has been changed, but what is deformed by sin is reformed by grace, not simply back to the state in integrity, but ultimately to a glorious state in the renewal of all things. The Reformed also insisted that man had a positive obligation to God's law written on his heart from the beginning. The negative probationary command provided a test of his attitude to God to the moral law: either God's word or man's insight.

Finally, Bavinck makes a further contribution concerning the realisation of the image of God in community under a representative head. 'It is not good that the man should be alone (Gen. 2:18); nor is it good that the man and woman should be alone. Upon the two of them God immediately pronounced the blessing of multiplication (Gen. 1:28). Not the man alone, nor the man and woman together, but only the whole of humanity is the fully developed image of God, his son, his offspring. The image of God is much too rich for it to be fully realised in a single human being however richly gifted that human being may be. It can only be somewhat unfolded in its depths and riches in a humanity counting billions of members.' Humanity is not a loose aggregate of individuals but an organism, one household, one family, united in one head. 'Only humanity in its entirety—as one complete organism, summed up under a single head, spread out over the whole earth, as prophet proclaiming the truth of God, as priest dedicating itself to God, as ruler controlling the earth and the whole of creation—only it is the fully finished image, the most telling and striking likeness of God.'

Bavinck confirms this from the descriptions of the church in the New Testament as the bride of Christ, the temple of the Holy Spirit etc. 'In both [the covenant of works and the covenant of grace] the goal and end is a kingdom of God, a holy humanity, in which God is all in all.'[5]

Humanity's unity in Adam is not simply a physical one but an ethical and spiritual one, and the same is true in Christ, the last Adam. The covenant of works and the covenant of grace stand and fall together. This has relevance to the origin of each soul. *Traducianism*, the theory that the soul is generated with the body, cannot account for the transmission of sin, which is an ethical or moral quality, not a physical one. On the other hand, *creationism*, the view that God directly creates each individual soul, while having its own difficulties, does not face this one, and has been preferred by Christians of the East and West other than Lutherans. While the soul is preformed in the psychic life of the unborn and receives its existence in the setting of sin which burdens the race, God elevates the psychic life to the level of the higher human spiritual life, in a

5 Herman Bavinck, *Reformed Dogmatics*, Vol 2., 578.

manner inexplicable to us, at some point between conception and birth.

23

THE COVENANT OF WORKS IN THE UNITED STATES

Covenant theology in America originated with settlers from lands where the Reformed and Presbyterian faith had found a hold—Scots/Irish, French, Dutch and Germans in particular. Those of the Congregational way in New England also were strongly attached to Covenant Theology, although quite early modifications occurred because civil rights were tied to church privileges. This led to an emphasis on historical faith as sufficient to qualify for church standing. In later reaction there was a strong emphasis on revival and on visible evidence of Christian standing.

America's remarkable preacher and greatest Christian thinker, **Jonathan Edwards** (1703–58), 'teaches just the "standard" Calvinism in its completeness', writes B.B.Warfield.[1] Considering Edwards drew on men like Ames, Wollebius, Turretin and **Peter Van Mastricht** (1630–1706), the successor at Utrecht to the great Gisbert Voetius (1589–1676), this is not surprising. In his notes

1 B.B.Warfield, 'Edwards and the New England Theology' in *Studies in Theology* (Oxford: Oxford University Press, 1932), 530. Peter Y. de Jong, *The Covenant Idea in New England Theology,* 1620–1847 (Grand Rapids: Eerdmans, 1945), 150f. argues otherwise but appears to tax Edwards with the views of some who used his name; cf. Paul Helm in the introduction to Jonathan Edwards, *Treatise on Grace,* (Cambridge: James Clarke & Co., 1971) 16f.

on Genesis 1:27–30, Edwards helpfully states the rationale of imputation:

> 'The blessings he [God] pronounces are given in the name of the whole race, and therefore the favour manifested in blessing them is implicitly given to him [Adam] as the head of the race... when Adam is threatened with being deprived of all these in case of his disobedience, Adam must understand it in like manner as a calamity to come upon the whole race, and consequently the implicit promise of life, as the confirmation of and increase of the blessing, respects also the whole race.'[2]

Edwards distinguished the covenant of redemption and the covenant of grace (contra Thomas Boston). His overall position is fair and square in the orthodox Reformed camp.[3]

American Presbyterian theologians commonly utilised Turretin as a standard text until the 1870s when local works were produced. **James H. Thornwell** (1812–62), a leading Presbyterian theologian in the South, has an extensive discussion on the covenant of works. He regards the covenant as essentially a conditioned promise, which man, in the exercise of his own free-will, might secure or forfeit. Thornwell characterises God's purpose as being to raise man from a servant to a son. This is a way of describing the advancement pledged in the covenant that does not seem to take account of the significance of Luke 3:31, which indicates Adam was already a son. Still, it is in essence a common viewpoint in the earlier period. Thornwell recognises God's grace in regard to the covenant, and

---

2 Edward Hickman (ed), *The Works of Jonathan Edwards, Vol 2* (Edinburgh: Bannner of Truth Trust, 1974), 689–690.

3 See Carl W. Bogue, *Jonathan Edwards and the Covenant of Grace* (Cherry Hill, NJ: Mack Publishing, 1975), 141–164.

that the reward of adoption would be a reward of grace as the fruit of man's obedience.[4]

The great **Charles Hodge** (1797–1878) based his own *Systematic Theology* (1871) on an adaptation of Turretin. He is quite brief on the covenant of works (6 pages, Vol. 2, 116–122). When discussing the saving work of Christ as the meritorious ground in justice for our salvation, Hodge reasons back to Adam using the language of merit in an unqualified way: 'Had Adam retained his integrity he would have merited the promised blessing.'[5] His son, A.A. Hodge (1823–86), sounds the usual note in 1879:

> 'It was also essentially a gracious covenant, because although every creature is, as such, bound to serve the creator to the full extent of his powers, the Creator cannot be bound as a mere matter of justice to grant the creature fellowship with himself.'[6]

In the *Systematic Theology* of **Robert Lewis Dabney** (1871, 1878), another Southerner, Turretin is quoted more than any other writer.[7] Dabney insists the creature cannot merit before God, affirms that God's act in entering into a covenant with Adam is one 'of pure grace and condescension' and that if he had obeyed he would have had graciously bestowed on him more than he had

4 James H. Thornwell, *The Collected Writings of James Henley Thornwell, Vol 1* (Edinburgh: Banner of Truth, 1974), 264ff.

5 Charles Hodge, *Systematic Theology*, Vol. 2 (London: Thomas Nelson, 1873), 364. Elsewhere Hodge goes against the Reformed consensus when he claims that Luke 17:10 does not prove a creature cannot perform an act which entitles to reward. 'God is just, and being just he rewards every man according to his works, so long as men are under the law.' (Vol. 3, 244)

6 A.A. Hodge, *Outlines of Theology* (1879 ed., London: Banner of Truth Trust, 1972); similarly, A.A. Hodge, *The Confession of Faith* (1869), 122.

7 Those most frequently cited were Turretin, Dick, Hill, Charles Hodge, Knapp, Watson, Ridgeley, Calvin, Thornwell and Witsius [so F.B.Lewis in David F. Wells (ed), *Southern Reformed Theology* (Grand Rapids: Baker, 1989), 57].

earned. He notes that a covenant with an indefinite probation would be no covenant at all, since the creature would be always liable to fall, and he uses the language of transfer from the position of a servant to a son, also found in Thornwell.[8]

W.G.T. Shedd (1820–94) of Union Seminary, New York, was another loyal adherent of the Westminster Confession. He states the classic position on merit succinctly: 'The merit to be acquired under the covenant of works was pactional. Adam could claim the reward, in case he stood, only by virtue of the promise of God; not by virtue of the original relation of a creature to the creator. Upon this latter basis he could claim nothing, as Christ teaches in Luke 17:10.'[9]

John L Girardeau (1825–98) was a renowned preacher and Professor of Theology at Columbia Theological Seminary, South Carolina 1876–95. In 1881, seeing the rise of departures from Covenant theology, he delivered an important lecture to the Alumni Association, entitled *The Federal Theology: Its Import and Regulative Influence.* This was republished in 1994 by Reformed Academic Press of Greenville, SC. Girardeau make a powerful and forceful case for the importance of the covenant of works. Adam as federal head meant 'his disobedience was the disobedience of the race, not subjectively and consciously but federally, legally and representatively'. Adam's posterity was not yet in existence but the guilt of Adam's sin was imputed to them immediately on the legal representation principle. Girardeau highlights the parallel with Christ as stated in Romans 5.

---

8 R.L. Dabney, *Systematic Theology* (St Louis: Presbyterian Publishing, 1878), 300–305.

9 W.G.T. Shedd, *Dogmatic Theology*, Vol 2 (Scribners, 1889), 153.

24

A RIVAL SYSTEM: THE RISE OF DISPENSATIONALISM

Dispensationalism is a system of thought particularly associated with names such as J.N. Darby (1800–82), C.I. Scofield (1843–1921) and L.S. Chafer (1871–1952). Chafer was the founder of what is now Dallas Theological Seminary. Dispensationalism was an increasingly accepted viewpoint in American evangelicalism from about 1880 onwards, and became deeply engrained among many evangelicals in the USA from the 1920s.

As defined by George W. Dollar:

> 'Dispensationalism is a system of Bible interpretation adhering to literalness in interpretation and distinguishing a series of periods in God's dealings with man in which God introduced a series of tests of responsibilities. In each of these tests of responsibilities man has proved an utter failure when left to himself and so has been thrust upon the grace of God for salvation. The commonly taught dividing points of the dispensations are the Fall, the Flood, the call of Abraham, the giving of the Law at Sinai, the Cross, the rapture of the Church and the tribulation.'[1]

---

1 G.W. Dollar, *A History of Fundamentalism in America* (Greenville: Bob Jones University Press, 1973), 279–340.

It will be seen that, as in classic Covenant Theology, there is an attempt to reckon with the historical unfolding of God's purposes. However, there are very significant differences between the two approaches. *First*, in Covenant Theology the emphasis falls on God's purpose with his creation. The covenant of creation and the covenant of grace have the same goal, the latter being the redemptive means to fulfil the first. The successive covenants are part of an organic whole. In the classic dispensational scheme the dispensations are different elements which lack a clear unifying factor. Indeed, they are often compartmentalised. Thus one can gain the impression that believers in the time of Moses were saved by law not by grace.

Comparison

Covenant Theology		Dispensational Theology	
1.	Adam	1.	Innocence (pre-fall)
2.	Noah	2.	Conscience (post fall)
3.	Abraham	3.	Human Government (post Flood)
4.	Moses	4.	Promise (grace)
5.	David	5.	Law (to Cross)
6.	Restoration	6.	Grace (from Cross onwards)
7.	Christ	7.	Kingdom (millennium)

Second, and very importantly, the dispensational scheme employs a radical literalism which leads to the view that God has separate and distinct purposes for Israel and the Church, the one earthly and the other heavenly. Israel in Scripture always means earthly Israel, it is claimed. Israel rejected the earthly Davidic kingdom offered her, and crucified her king. Consequently, the Lord, through the Apostles, introduced the Church age with a heavenly message for the Gentiles. This parenthesis will continue until God again renews the kingdom to ethnic Israel during an earthly millennium. Before that happens the gospel must be preached to all the nations as a testimony, but a pessimism about both its reception and the faithfulness of the organised church is characteristic. A great tribulation will precede the millennium, but the church will be raptured away to heaven before it occurs.

On the other hand, Covenant Theology sees the choice of Israel as part of God's preparation for the coming of Christ when salvation would be proclaimed among the nations. The kingdom of Israel was intended to provide an illustration of the kingdom of God inaugurated by Christ, just as surely as the sacrificial system provided types of Christ's saving work. Old Testament promises about the future employed the images of the institutions of Israel without at all meaning to limit the fulfilment to a mere earthly reproduction of them. The notion that the Old Testament promises are fulfilled other than in and through the church as the new/expanded Israel of God is anathema. The unity of the church in every age is basic. Literal interpretation means the intended meaning not the literalistic meaning.

How Did the Dispensational Teaching Arise?

Some of the soil which gave dispensationalism birth may be seen in the over-literal interpretation of Scripture, particularly unfulfilled prophecy, dating from Puritan times. Reformed churches had generally taken over Augustine's view which saw no special future millennial period. The Reformed commonly did anticipate a future conversion of the Jews, based on Romans 11:26, and they held a positive view of the future of the gospel in the world.[2] Their

2 One could note the 'Dutch Annotations' of 1637 prepared by the authority of the Synod of Dordt as in the same vein as the generality of British theologians of the

interpretative principle was broadly historicist, and the Roman Antichrist and the rise of Islam were regarded as among those events predicted in the Book of Revelation which had already been fulfilled. Influential men offered dates for the fulfilment of various predictions.

In the 1640s one finds many prophetic discussions occurring in Britain, and a revival of the old pre-millennial scheme which held that Christ in some sense would reign over the earth for 1000 years from Jerusalem.[3] However, the excesses of the Fifth Monarchy men contributed to the pre-millennial viewpoint taking a notable back seat in subsequent generations. **Daniel Whitby** (1638–1726), an English Anglican who was by no means a Calvinist in theology, furthered this trend.

In 1703 Whitby published his *A Treatise of the True Millennium: Shewing that it is not a Reign of Persons Raised from the Dead, but of the Church Flourishing Gloriously for a Thousand Years after the Conversion of the Jews and the Flowing in of all Nations to them thus Converted to the Christian Faith*[4]. In it, he rejected any notion of the Jews rebuilding the temple, but did not rule out a restoration to their own land.[5] His significance is his use of Revelation 20 in the service of a post-millennial viewpoint. The millennium was a future period in which the gospel would so flourish that Christianity would cover the earth and after (post) this millennium Christ would return. Most earlier writers, and all the Puritan

period. They were translated into English and published in London in 1657.

3 A fine survey is Crawford Gribben, 'The Eschatology of the Puritan Confessions' in *Scottish Bulletin of Evangelical Theology* 20:1 (Spring 2002), 51–78. See also my essay 'Christian Mission to the Jews 1550–1850' in Paul Morris (ed.), *The Gospel and Israel* (Eugene, OR: Wipf & Stock, 2014), 102–125.

4 Included as an appendix to his *A paraphrase and commentary on the New Testament* (London 1703).

5 Daniel Whitby, *A paraphrase…*, 259.

confessions, had avoided citing this passage in support of their views. During the 18th century post-millennial historicism was the common viewpoint, and the argument from fulfilled prophecies was widely utilised to provide proofs of the truth of Christianity against prevailing unbelief. People as eminent as Jonathan Edwards anticipated the possibility of the millennium beginning in their own times.

In the nature of the case historicism was vulnerable in the event of major social or political developments raising questions about its predictions. The French Revolution of 1789 was just such an event, and caused a flurry of debate about what it meant for prophetic history and for society, given that post-millennial thought was utilised to promote right behaviour and the expectation of the ultimate overthrow of Roman Catholicism. In the Irish context of rebellion in 1798 and 1803, and then the Napoleonic wars, the millennial influences on Anglican curate **J.N. Darby** were considerable. Over against the current emphasis on this world's transformation, he took a pessimistic view and emphasised a dualism that gave earthly hopes to ethnic Israel, but reserved the heavenly vision of God for the Church considered as the separated and holy bride of Christ.[6] He embraced a premillennial viewpoint, but with the rapture of the saints before the great tribulation he expected. The teaching of a pre-tribulation rapture has no history before about 1827 when it was allegedly revealed by a person in Darby's circle who purported to exercise the gift of prophecy. The failure of the Millerite prediction of the second advent for 1843/44, accelerated the rejection of historicism in favour of futurism. In

---

6 Note the important article by Gary L. Nebeker should be consulted: 'John Nelson Darby and Trinity College, Dublin: A Study in Eschatological Contrasts' in *Fides et Historia*, XXIV.2 (Summer/Fall 2002), 87–108.

the course of time, Darby's views were elaborated into a theory of different dispensations, and enshrined in the *Scofield Reference Bible* first published in 1909.

Did Covenant Theology Prepare the Way?

It is evident that dispensationalism did not arise in a vacuum, but only a superficial reading will credit Covenant Theology as its forerunner. We have seen earlier that there were differences about the Mosaic covenant in the 1640s. Even the majority who claimed it was a dispensation of grace acknowledged it had a legal aspect which looked like a covenant of works, and a minority actually regarded it as a covenant of works although subservient to the covenant of grace. A look at this dualistic tendency is in order.

In 1742 the hymn-writer and English Independent, **Isaac Watts** (1674–1748) issued a modest book entitled *The harmony of all the religions which God ever prescribed: containing a brief survey of the several publick dispensations of God toward man, or his appointment of different forms of religion in successive ages, humbly proposed as an easy clew to lead us through many difficulties of the Old Testament, and the New* ..[7] The title reflects the reality that there was still a lack of clarity on the covenants among ordinary Christians. Watts outlines his understanding of the successive stages of the covenant of grace through Adam–Noah–Abraham –Moses and Christ. In regard to the Mosaic dispensation, Watts recognises the covenant of grace in it, but also speaks of some of the outward precepts and ordinances making up what he calls 'the peculiar Sinai covenant' which separated the Jews from other nations. In nature this

7 Isaac Watts, *The Harmony of All Religion* ... (London: pr. for J. Brackstone), xii + 102pp.

peculiar covenant was a covenant of works (cf. Deut. 6:2–25), but it related to temporal blessings in the land of Canaan not to spiritual blessings and eternal salvation. It was a 'temporal appendix' to the covenant of grace by which God as King ruled the nation, and 'was not designed to reach to the concerns of another world'. It was the fault of the Jews to mistake the way of justification on the temporal level (works) with the way of justification on the spiritual level (faith).

A viewpoint along this line is found in the earlier period, as we have seen although it was a minority one. However, it gives no support to classic dispensational teaching on the radically different program of God for Israel. Still, in so far as the subject was difficult to explain with simplicity and clarity, alternative explanations could gain a foothold.[8]

The discussions on infant baptism in the 1640s and later are not irrelevant. Some of Baptist leanings were inclined to regard the covenant with Abraham as a mixed covenant also: the natural seed of Abraham inherited temporal benefits and the spiritual seed gospel blessings.[9] By this distinction the covenant membership of children in the Old Testament was related to the temporal aspect not the spiritual, so removing an argument for the covenant

8 Note a comment by John Owen, *Epistle to the Hebrews*, Vol. 6, 87 on a related Roman Catholic view: 'I cannot but somewhat admire how it came into the heart or mind of any man to think or say, that God ever gave a law or laws, precept or precepts, that "should respect the outward man only, and the regulation of external duties." A thought of it is contrary to all the essential properties of the nature of God… The life and foundation of all the laws under the old testament was, "Thou shalt love the LORD thy God with all thy soul;" without which no outward obedience was ever accepted with him.'

9 John Tombes, *Two treatises and an appendix to them concerning Infant-Baptisme. The former being a Exercitation presented to the Chairman of a Committee of the Assembly of Divines*… translated out of the Latin by the author (London, December 15, 1645), 2.

membership of the children of New Testament believers based on Old Testament precedent.

The influence of this dualism can also be noted in others such as the able Baptist Dr **John Gill** (1697–1771). He writes of the covenant with Adam (1769): 'It contained a promise; which was a promise of life, of natural life to Adam, and a continuation of it so long as he should observe the condition of it; just as life was promised to the Israelites, and a continuation of it, in the land of Canaan, so long as they should observe the law of God; for neither the law of Moses, nor the law of nature, made promise of any other than of a natural life. Some divines, and those of great name and figure in the churches of Christ, think, and indeed it is most generally received, that Adam continuing in his obedience, had a promise of eternal life. I cannot be of that mind.'[10] Gill's reasons seem largely to derive from his belief that, as eternal life is the gift of God in Christ according to the eternal covenant, and as life and immortality have been brought to light through the gospel, then eternal life or any spiritual blessing could not have been promised to Adam before the fall.

In the work of another Baptist, **Abraham Booth** (1734–1806), something similar is at work. Concerning his *Essay on the Kingdom of Christ* (1788) it has been said: 'Mr. Booth's Essay is a scriptural illustration of the subject, designed to show that as the kingdom of Christ is not of this world, it must in its nature be different from that of the kingdom of David, and the entire constitution of things under the Jewish theocracy. Hence he justly infers that it is quite absurd to reason from what took place under the Mosaic economy,

10 John Gill, *A Body of Divinity* (Grand Rapids: Sovereign Grace 1971) Book 3, Ch. VII, p. 314.

to the nature of the Christian church, and the rights, privileges, and duties of the subjects of the Messiah's kingdom, since these are as different as flesh and spirit, temporal and spiritual.'[11]

These tendencies, combined with reaction to worldliness in the church, certainly made it easier for the 19th century to dispense with Covenant Theology's insistence on continuity between Old and New Testaments. Happily, particularly since the publication of the *New Scolfield Reference Bible* in 1967, there is a growing school of progressive dispensationalists who, while retaining premillennialism, modify a number of the older positions in a more satisfactory direction.[12]

11 Memoir prefixed to some editions of Booth's *Reign of Grace*, his most popular work.

12 A good introduction is Craig A. Blaising & Darrell L. Bock, *Progressive Dispensationalism* (Grand Rapids: Baker, 2000).

25

COVENANT THEOLOGY IN THE 20TH CENTURY

In the English-speaking world orthodox Covenant Theology has not been prominent in the 20th century, but has had a more sustained life in areas of Dutch influence. This reflects its eclipse in Britain in the 1870s, as either liberal or more general evangelical views took over, but the renewal of Calvinistic thought in the Netherlands which began around the same time (although now in steep decline). The neo-orthodoxy of **Karl Barth** (1886–1968) has been influential and has had its impact in the formulations of more orthodox interpreters.

The Adamic covenant of works was recognised among subscribers to the Westminster Confession, but not a great deal was made of it except in small pockets, as at Westminster Theological Seminary in Philadelphia. Although Reformed theology had carefully qualified the 'merit' category and stressed 'grace' in the pre-fall relationship in the sense of love, kindness and assistance, clarity in regard to Adam's original status as a son has only come into its own in the 20th century.

Covenant theology was a living part of church life in many Dutch circles, but the lack of explicit reference in the Dutch Confessions did not help the maintenance of the basic contours that were once universal among them. Indeed, in reaction to the views of **Abraham Kuyper** (1837–1920) which, on the covenant of works, were in the traditional line, but not always well nuanced,[1] there was a general move away from seeing the pre-fall arrangement as a probation envisaging the blessing of eternal life. Kuyper's formulation was seen as somewhat scholastic and of a piece with other distinctions he made which created great controversy, namely, his teaching of presumed regeneration as the ground of infant baptism. So discussions in the last 50 years on the covenant have not been in the setting of justification, nor have they typically been well informed on the classic period of Reformed theology in the 17th century. Even the greatest of the Dutch theologians, Herman Bavinck tends to be overlooked. The somewhat modified views of Klaas Schilder influenced many.

Objections to Terminology

G.H. Kersten (1882–1948), the chief instrument in the forming of the *Gereformeerde Gemeenten* (Reformed Congregations) in 1907, published his *Reformed Dogmatics* in 1947. As might be expected

1 Note this comment on the Heidelberg Catechism (Lord's Day 24) which is an elaboration of the emphasis in some earlier theologians, but more starkly put: 'In the covenant of works the children of men are hired servants who serve for wages, and when they provide their service have a right to their reward. They expect that reward because God has given them the privilege to expect it. The redeemed in Christ do not come as hired servants but as children in a family. To perceive the difference between the two you have to notice the difference in your own home between a servant and a child. The hired servant negotiates pay, has to work for that pay, and when she has completed her task receives her pay. Completely different is the status of a child in the family. Such a child also works, but simply because the father or mother has given him a task, and it is a joy for the child to work with the father or mother. Though the children do not get any reward they still work.' *E Voto Dordraceno, Vol. 2* (Amsterdam 1895) 389. The translation is by Rev Cor Vanderhorn of Sunshine Presbyterian Church, Melbourne. G.C.Berkouwer, *Studies in Dogmatics: Sin* (Grand Rapids: Eerdmans, 1971) 207fn. also cites Kuyper's *Uit het Woord II*, 209, but this reference is not correct.

of this conservative, experiential denomination with roots in the Secession of the 1830s, Kersten follows the lines of the classic Reformed position as exampled by the Westminster Confession and Alexander Comrie. He recognises that the covenant of grace revealed God's goodness and love to man and has no problems with the term 'covenant of works'.[2] A recent writer who doesn't shrink from the traditional covenant of works terminology is **Donald Macleod** of the Free Church of Scotland College, Edinburgh. Macleod writes: 'There is nothing inherently improper in a covenant of works. Our very salvation rests on the obedience of the Last Adam and that obedience was compliance with a covenant of works. Christ saved us by finishing the work given him to do (John 17:4). He was 'obedient unto death' (Phil. 2:8). 'By the obedience of the one shall many be made righteous' (Rom. 5:19). There were indeed gracious elements in the covenant of works. But we must accept that the primary relationship between God and man is a relationship of works and obedience.'[3]

But others did scruple the terminology. In the 1930s, **S.G. de Graaf** (1889–1955), the famous Amsterdam preacher, introduced the expression 'covenant of favour' because he did not believe the expression 'of works' did justice to the pre-redemptive grace in the covenant: 'We are accustomed to speaking of this covenant as the covenant of works. However, we should not take this name to mean that man was expected to earn eternal life as a reward for doing good works, as though eternal life was man's payment

---

2 G.H. Kersten, *Reformed Dogmatics, Vol. 1* (Grand Rapids: Netherlands Reformed, 1980), 192–208.

3 Donald Macleod, *A Faith to Live By* (Fearn: Christian Focus, 2002) 122. Macleod does not stress an eschatological aspect to the promise of life, cf. also his article 'Federal Theology: An Oppressive Legalism?' in *The Banner of Truth*, 125 (February 1974) 22.

for services rendered. Because man owes everything he is and has to God, we may never speak of man earning wages paid out by God. Therefore it might be wiser to speak of the covenant of God's favour...'[4] Similarly, **Klaas Schilder** (1890–1952) considered that the contrast of works and faith had caused much confusion, as if there was no favour before the fall and that man could earn his salvation.[5] **G.C.Berkouwer** (1903–1996) also agreed with de Graaf's critique: the suggestion that God has favour on man only after his obedience and not at the beginning, implied God's favour, love and communion did not exist at the very beginning. It would follow that the terrible reality of man's guilt is lessened, and also lead us to think of man as originally in an impersonal legalistic relationship with God.[6] Berkouwer to some extent was influenced by Barth.

Cornelis Vander Waal (1919–1980), a disciple of Schilder, maintained that God's covenant existed with pre-fall Adam, but he rejected the idea of a covenant of works since he regarded it as implying merit. He pointedly stated: 'Adam was not created to be a legitimate Pharisee, pelagian, or remonstrant.'[7] In common with others he seems to confuse obedience with the notion of inherent merit.

---

4 S.G. de Graaf, *Promise and Deliverance, Vol 1* (St Catherines, Ont.: Paedia Press, 1977), 37. This is a translation by H.E. and E.W. Runner of the original work published in 1937 as *Verbondsgeschiedenis.*

5 *Het Verbond in de Gereformeerde Symbolen*, van Prof. Dr. K. Schilder, Collegeverslagen Symboliek Cursus 1944–1945, Verslag en uitgave geheel buiten verantwoordelijkheid van Prof.Schilder, 2e druk. [The Covenant in the Reformed Symbols, by Prof. Dr. K. Schilder, Notes of Lectures in Symbolics, Course 1944-1945. Prof. Schilder does not take any responsibility for this report and publication. 2nd edition.] The compilers were two students: N. Bruin and C. van Venetie. I owe this reference to Rev. Gerald van Rongen of Kelmscott, Western Australia.

6 G.C. Berkouwer, *Sin*, 207–208. This is a translation of the 1958 Dutch original.

7 *The Covenantal Gospel* (Neerlandia, Alb.: Inheritance Publishers, 1990), 54.

Outside Dutch circles, **John Murray** (1898–1975), Professor of Theology at Westminster Seminary in Philadelphia 1930–66, also objected to the term covenant of works: 'There are two observations. (1) The term is not felicitous, for the reason that the elements of grace entering into the administration are not properly provided for by the term 'works'. (2) It is not designated a covenant in Scripture. Hosea 6:7 may be interpreted otherwise and does not provide the basis for such a construction of the Adamic economy. Besides, Scripture always uses the term covenant, when applied to God's administration to men, in reference to a provision that is redemptive or closely related to redemptive design. Covenant in Scripture denotes the oath-bound confirmation of promise and involves a security which the Adamic economy did not bestow.'[8]

It is in the last two sentences quoted that Murray's distinctive viewpoint appears. However, under the term 'the Adamic Administration' he admitted the substance of the classic Reformed position even if he rejected the terminology. I have not seen any discussion by Murray on the exegesis that finds a covenant relation with creation from the beginning vide Jeremiah 33:20ff and Genesis 9:6 and 6:18 (see pages 15–16). Perhaps if he had considered this he may have modified his presentation. A weakness of Murray's presentation is the tendency of some to move further along the line he suggested and away altogether from the idea of a pre-fall arrangement with a conditional promise of eternal life.

Those making the objections stated can be taken as wanting (a) to allow for some kind of (non-redemptive) grace, favour or

8 *Collected Writings of John Murray, Vol. 2* (Edinburgh: Banner of Truth Trust, 1977), 49. A.A.Hoekema, *Created in God's Image* (Grand Rapids: Eerdmans, 1986), 117–121, whose 1953 PhD was on Herman Bavinck's *Doctrine of the Covenant*, surprisingly follows largely Murray's line.

goodness in the pre-fall context, and (b) to reject the concept of merit as if it permitted man to earn something from God. Here they are perfectly in line with all the early writers. However, to the extent there is confusion or under-emphasis on the requirement of perfect obedience as the condition of the promised life, as is the case in some of the Dutch, there is an opening made for major problems.

A Covenantal Creation

One point on which a rather general agreement is forming is that of the nature of the pre-fall, pre-Genesis 2:16–17 state of Adam. The tendency of some of the 17th century theologians to contrast a state of nature prior to the covenant state and to associate that initial state with a relatively servile position is rather widely accepted as failing to do justice to the biblical data. Far too often the original state of Adam before the covenant of Genesis 2 has been characterised inadequately. Even **Wayne Grudem** felt able to write recently: 'Nor did the nature of man as God created him demand that God have any fellowship with man or that God make any promises concerning his relationship with men, or give man any clear directions concerning what he should do.'[9]

The idea of the initial state of creation being covenantal is found in American Presbyterian/Reformed writers such as

9 Wayne Grudem, *Systematic Theology* (Leicester, UK: IVP, 1994) 517. Robert L. Reymond's rather uneven *A New Systematic Theology of the Christian Faith* (Nashville: Nelson, 1998), 416 is not quite clear on man in covenant prior to the explicit arrangement of Genesis 2:16–17, but Reymond does avoid contrasting the two pre-fall states in a starkly polarised way.

Cornelius Van Til,[10] **Meredith Kline**,[11] **O. Palmer Robertson**,[12] **Morton H. Smith**[13] and Anglicans such as **William Dumbrell**.[14] These men see the arrangement of Genesis 2 as, in Smith's words, 'a particularisation of the Covenant, which was designed to bring man to self-conscious choice and realisation of his covenant relation with God.'

The neo-Kuyperian writer, **Gordon Spykman** (1926–93) writes similarly: 'The covenant is rooted in God's work of creation. God covenanted his world into existence. Covenantal relationships are given in, with and for all created reality. From the beginning creation is unthinkable apart from its covenantal relationship of dependence and responsiveness *coram Deo*. Though the word "covenant" does not appear in the creation account (Gen. 1, 2), the basic elements of classical covenant making are clearly present. They are evident in (a) the preamble with its prologue, introducing the Sovereign in his relationship to the second party, (b) the promises and obligations which define the community established by the covenantal pact, and (c) the blessing-and-curse formula, with its stated condition for fidelity and its stated penalty for infidelity.'[15]

---

10 Cornelius Van Til, "Nature and Scripture" in *The Infallible Word: A Symposium by members of the Faculty of Westminster Theological Seminary,* ed. N. B. Stonehouse et al (Philadelphia: Presbyterian & Reformed Publishing Co., 1967), 267. This section is unchanged from the first edition in 1946. Van Til writes: 'Being from the outset covenantal in character, the natural revelation of God to man was meant to serve as the playground for the process of differentiation that was to take place in the course of time.'

11 M.G. Kline, *By Oath Consigned* (Grand Rapids: Eerdmans, 1968) 19, 36–37

12 O. Palmer Robertson, *The Christ of the Covenants* (Phillipsburg, NJ: Presbyterian & Reformed, 1980); *Covenants: God's way with his people* (Philadelphia: Great Commission, 1987).

13 Morton H. Smith, *Systematic Theology, Vol. 1* (Greenville, SC: Greenville Seminary Press, 1994), 280.

14 W.J. Dumbrell, *Covenant and Creation* (Carlisle, UK: Paternoster, 1984).

15 G.J. Spykman, *Reformational Theology* (Grand Rapids: Eerdmans, 1992), 260.

Similarly, **J. Van Genderen** and **W.H. Velema**, professors of the conservative *Christian Reformed Churches in the Netherlands* write: 'In Genesis 2:17 we read of a prohibition which is accompanied by a sanction, while the tree of life reminds of the blessing of life, which man will receive, if he does not transgress the prohibition.... Just as "being the image of God" indicates that the relationship with God is not an arbitrary or voluntary relation, so one may say that everything which follows thereon displays the character of a covenant, even if it is not explicitly said so.... The relation of God to man is in essence a covenant relationship. The elements are present, the term not. It is not a construction from our side when we point out the elements in Genesis 1 and 2. On the contrary, we do no more than retrace biblical lines and connect them with each other. We prefer to speak of a "covenant of life" (Smaller Catechism) instead of a "covenant of works".'[16]

The Barthian/Torrance school

The school of **Karl Barth** (1886–1968), the neo-orthodox existential theologian, has opposed traditional Covenant Theology as an oppressive legalism. Of course, Barthianism does not hold to the historical reality of the fall of man in Adam: each person is his/her own Adam. The particularism of redemptive grace is rejected in place of a virtual universalism. In the hands of exponents such as **James B. Torrance** (1923–2003) and **Holmes Rolston III**

16 *Beknopte Gereformeerde Dogmatiek* (Kampen: Kok, 1992) 363. This work [*Concise Reformed Dogmatics*] is widely used in both the CGKN and the GKN(V). The translation was supplied by Rev R.C.Janssen of Nagele, the Netherlands and for substance is as in the English translation entitled *Concise Reformed Dogmatics* (Phillipsburg: P & R, 2008), 395–396.

(b.1932),[17] there has been a sustained critique of the theology of the covenants of works and grace. Developments subsequent to Calvin have been seen as a betrayal of his position which, strange to tell, is represented as Barthian. One can readily admit some unfortunate phraseology and abstractions in the formulations of the covenant theologians. However, the heart of the critique is uninformed, unhistorical and unjustified biblically.

1. Barthians argue that the Adamic covenant as historically understood is one that gives priority to law rather than grace. In doing so they refuse to admit that redemptive grace only has its proper meaning in the context of disobedience to law, nor do they face up to the fact that the strictly orthodox always acknowledged that before the fall there was 'grace' for the righteous Adam in the sense of love, favour and assistance.

2. This school claims that merit is not an appropriate category in the Adamic relationship. However, it is not self-evident that merit in a certain sense is inappropriate to the relationship. Certainly the historic position in reformed theology defined merit in terms of God's faithfulness to his covenant promise, and all but universally rejected the notion of merit as wages for obedience by Adam.

3. When the Torrance critique stigmatises the traditional formulation as a mere contract, it forgets that the contract idea is inherently involved in a covenant, which is an agreement with

17 K. Barth, *Church Dogmatics IV.1*, 22–66; J.B.Torrance has repeatedly written on the theme with covenant or contract as the polarised choices, e.g. 'The Contribution of McLeod Campbell to Scottish Theology' in *Scottish Journal of Theology* 26 (1973), 295–311; Holmes Rolston, *John Calvin versus the Westminster Confession* (Richmond, VA: John Knox Press, 1972); For a fine critique of J.B.Torrance's position see Donald Macleod's article in *Dictionary of Scottish Church History and Theology* (Edinburgh: T. & T. Clark, 1993), 217–218.

mutual obligations, even if it cannot exhaust the nature of the covenant as a bond between friends and lovers.

The contribution of Meredith Kline

Meredith Kline (1922–2007), who trained under Murray, and was Professor of Old Testament at Westminster 1948–65, initially followed the Murray line. He diverged as a result of his Old Testament study, and the light cast by studies in ancient Hittite treaties. These suggested to him that Murray's equation of covenant with 'sovereign administration of grace and promise' was inadequate as some of these covenants included a works principle.[18] As of 1968, he held a rather standard WCF position, speaking of voluntary condescension in the making of the covenant with Adam, although in the setting of a covenantal creation (as already noted).[19] Kline preferred the term Covenant of Creation, since there are works under the redemptive covenant as well as the pre-redemptive. By 1980, his views had sharpened, no doubt in part due to tendencies he considered detrimental to a sound Reformed position which were circulating, including the position of Norman Shepherd, Murray's successor at Westminster 1962–81.

1. Kline draws a strict parallel between Adam and Christ, and insists on merit as a proper category in both cases. He rightly rejects any human righteousness as an autonomous possession or achievement, and any abstract definition of justice. He defines merit as what accords to strict justice, but insists that what is just is what is revealed in God's covenant.[20] These are

18 Rev. C. Lee Irons personal communication to R.S.Ward 22 February 2003, recalling conversations with Dr Kline in the late 1990s.

19 M.G.Kline, *By Oath Consigned* (Grand Rapids: Eerdmans, 1968) 19, 36–37.

20 For advocacy of this view see C. Lee Irons, 'Redefining Merit: An

tighter positions than were usual for the 17th century writers, but certainly do not imperil the doctrine of justification but the reverse. In my estimation Kline is really very close to the classic position. It holds God was bound to reward man because of what God pledged in covenant if the man was obedient. In regard to the parallel between Adam and Christ, both stand in a covenant relation with the Father as sons, but although there are similarities there are differences. The First Adam stood in holy communion and love with God, and sin was not in the equation. There was no demerit to contend with, whereas Jesus, the Last Adam, had to bear the sin and demerit of those he represented. Thus the older writers would freely use the language of merit for Christ's work, but carefully qualify it for Adam's.

2. Contrary to his position in 1968, Kline does not wish now to admit any concept of 'grace' in the pre-fall relationship lest it cloud the reality that life was to be gained only in the way of obedience. After all, Christ finished the work he was given to do and claimed the reward on that account.

The classic position recognised (non-redemptive) grace or favour in the pre-fall relationship, but nevertheless insisted that faithful obedience was required, and that God had by covenant bound himself to reward it. Kline's concern is to avoid undermining the necessity of Christ's active obedience in our place, and modifying the nature of justification, a major issue in the current theological climate. This concern is valid, but admitting what the

Examination of Medieval Presuppositions in Covenant Theology' in Howard Griffith and John R. Muether *Creator, Redeemer, Consummator: A Festschrift for Meredith G. Kline* (Greenville, SC: Reformed Academic Press/Reformed Theological Seminary, 2000), 253–69.

virtually unanimous voice of Reformed theology has regarded as scriptural for 400 years is hardly likely to open the floodgates to error. Concern about other influences, such as Barthianism, is surely affecting Kline's formulation (see below).

3. Kline also offers a view of the works element in the Mosaic covenant that has the works-inheritance principle operating on the earthly and temporal level but not in the spiritual sphere. Whatever one thinks of this Isaac Watts type view, it should be able to be discussed on its merits. Of course, one must always remember that the land was not given to Israel because she was righteous (Deut. 9:4,6), and that the obedience required by Israel was the obedience that flowed from her redemption by the Lord (Exod. 19:3ff.). As has been shown in Chapter 18, stating the niceties of the Mosaic covenant has not been found easy.[21]

Non-eschatological views

Herman Hoeksema (1886–1964) was another of Dutch background who objected strongly to the idea of a covenant of works, since he held that a covenant relationship existed from the beginning. Always too, in Hoeksema, one sees the covenant viewed

21 M.G.Kline, *Images of the Spirit* (Grand Rapids: Baker, 1980) 23. *Kingdom Prologue: Genesis Foundations for a Covenantal Worldview* (Two Age Press, 2000), pp. 1–7, 14–21, 107–17, 138–42. Also 'Gospel until the Law: Rom 5:13–14 and the Old Covenant' in *Journal of the Evangelical Theological Society* 34 (1991) 433–446. Kline's positions have been championed by Mark W. Karlberg, but his contribution has been blunted by misplaced argument and very personal attacks on others, particularly Norman Shepherd and those perceived to sympathise with the latter's position. Many of Karlberg's articles are in M. W. Karlberg, *Covenant Theology in Reformed Perspective* (Eugene, OR.: Wipf & Stock, 2000); A bitter attack on Westminster Seminary in Philadelphia is in his *The Changing of the Guard* (Unicoi, Tenn.: The Trinity Review, 2001). Dr Richard Gaffin's position is in fact in the line of H. Bavinck and G. Vos, as is my own.

from the standpoint of election. Hoeksema affirmed: 'From the very first moment of his existence, therefore, and in virtue of his being created after the image of God, Adam stood in that covenant relation to God, and was conscious of that living fellowship and friendship which is essential to that relationship.'[22]So far so good. However, Hoeksema proceeded (1) to reject the notion of a post-creation, pre-fall covenant, since he considered that it would make the covenant relation something incidental and additional rather than essential; (2) to affirm the arrangement in Genesis 2 is simply a command not the covenant; and (3) to reject the idea that a promise of eternal life in glory can be deduced from the threat of death.

In his rejection of the traditional covenant of works Hoeksema displays a poor grasp of the classic position, and places it in a bad light. He cites only Charles Hodge, characterises the traditional viewpoint as involving the notion of the inherent merit of the creature (a virtually universally rejected position), and as implying a servile position for man pre-fall.[23] Unhappily, the language has often suggested this latter point as we have seen. Hoeksema's main departure is in the rejection of an eschatology before sin, and thus of any probationary idea. The same reservation is made by **G.C.Berkouwer**[24], and others such as **Henri Blocher**[25],

---

22 H. Hoeksema, *The Triple Knowledge, Vol 1* (Grand Rapids: Reformed Free Publishing, 1972), 116. This part of Hoeksema's work was first published in 1943.

23 Hoeksema, *The Triple Knowledge, Vol 1*, 103–113.

24 G.C. Berkouwer, *Studies in Dogmatics: Man, the Image of God* (Grand Rapids: Eerdmans 1962), 345. This is a translation of the 1957 Dutch original. Contrast Geerhardus Vos [1862–1949], *The Pauline Eschatology* (Princeton, NJ, 1930), 304: 'The only reasonable interpretation of the Genesis-account (*e mente Pauli*) [according to the mind of Paul] is this, that provision was made and probation was instituted for a still higher state, both ethico-religiously and physically complexioned, than was at that time in the possession of man.'

25 H. Blocher, *In the Beginning* (Downers Grove: IVP, 1984), 133.

and **Clarence Stam.**[26] It will be recalled that the Westminster Confession does not define the life promised in the covenant of works and that there were differences on that point. One can hardly stigmatise the rejection of the idea of Adamic probation as confessionally unorthodox, but the failure to contrast law and grace appropriately certainly is.

Klaas Schilder (already noted on page 208) reacted against distinctions that seemed artificial and unbiblical, such as were characteristic of aspects of Kuyper's theology. Schilder and others tended to flatten out the difference between the covenant pre-fall and the covenant post-fall. In reaction to Kuyper grounding baptism on presumptive regeneration (raising the question of baptism's significance if the child grew up and rejected the faith), Schilder insisted on the objective reality of God's promise to the baptised and stressed the obligations in the covenant. In this scenario emphasis is on one covenant requiring faithful obedience by man throughout. Indeed, whereas Hoeksema viewed the covenant through election, Schilder's approach saw election through the covenant, which risked self-assurance and legalism ('being in the church I am also of the church'). Neither position represents the older view which reckoned with the administration of the covenant of grace in a two-fold sense: baptism is grounded on God's command and promise and all who profess the true religion together with their children are reckoned in the covenant outwardly; however, strictly speaking it is only those united to Christ by grace through faith who receive the saving benefits of the covenant.

---

26 Clarence Stam, *The Covenant of Love* (Winnipeg: Premier Publishing, 1999), 49–50.

Let Stam be our illustration: Stam's book, *The Covenant of Love*, is a pastorally sensitive work by a minister of the Canadian Reformed Churches. Stam does not think of the covenant as a means of advancing humanity to greater blessing, and he actually rejects such an idea. There is no reference in his book to such a crucial passage as 1 Corinthians 15:42–49, and Stam supposes Adam was perfect in an ideal sense, not needing advancement. Rather, we have a single covenant of love made with Adam requiring faithful obedience, the formal distinction of covenant of works and covenant of grace being discarded. Also, very strikingly, Stam does not explain the results of Adam's sin in terms of imputation. Indeed, the imputation of Christ's righteousness and the central truth of justification by his perfect obedience to God's law are not given quite the emphasis one would expect. There is no reference to Romans 5:12ff. Stam believes the Heidelberg Catechism, but his own presentation is rather different from its authors or from orthodox expositors in earlier times.

One is reminded of the words of the old Dutch writer, Wilhelmus à Brakel: 'Acquaintance with this covenant [of works] is of the greatest importance, for whoever errs here or denies the existence of the covenant of works will not understand the covenant of grace, and will readily err concerning the mediatorship of the Lord Jesus. Such a person will very readily deny that Christ by His active obedience has merited a right to eternal life for the elect.'[27]

27 W. à Brakel, *The Christian's Reasonable Service* [1700] (Ligonier: Soli Deo Gloria, 1992) Vol 1, 355. One could add that there are parallels in modern trends with the position of Richard Baxter (1615–1691), a great practical theologian but a disaster as a systematic theologian. He published his *Aphorismes on Justification* in 1649. Reacting against the antinomian views in his time he went to the opposite extreme, and taught that following the breaking of the covenant of works God established a

Norman Shepherd (b. 1933), Murray's successor at Westminster Seminary 1962–81, holds a similar position to Stam, although he sees the command with respect to the tree of the knowledge of good and evil as a kind of probation. His short book, *The Call of Grace*, is not comprehensive, and he has kindly outlined his covenant theology thus[28]:

1. Adam was created in covenant with the Lord God.
2. Covenant defines a divinely established relationship of union and communion between God and his people maintained in the bonds of mutual love and faithfulness. This description covers all of the historical covenants beginning with Adam (Adamic, Noahic, Abrahamic, Mosaic, Davidic, and New).
3. As in all covenants so also in the Adamic covenant there are two parts, promise and obligation.
4. God gives life to Adam (God made Adam a living creature in his own image for fellowship with himself), and promises life to him comparable to the eternal life we now anticipate through faith in Jesus Christ.
5. God pledges his love and faithfulness to his covenant partner and seeks for the same love and faithfulness in return. Adam is his image bearer and is created and designed to reflect the excellencies of his Father in heaven.
6. Since life is promised as a gift and not as something to be achieved or merited by the performance of good works, it is to be received by faith.

---

covenant of grace which was really a new covenant of works on more easy terms. In effect it made our faith in Christ's righteousness and not Christ's righteousness itself, the ground of our acceptance with God. This 'neo-nomian' influence with its legalistic approach impacted Scotland in the early 1700s ultimately leading to the reaction of the Marrow Controversy.

28 Personal communication by N. Shepherd to R.S.Ward, 4 March 2003. *The Call of Grace* (Phillipsburg: P & R. Publishing, 2000).

7. God created Adam to be a righteous man who would live now and forever by faith.
8. The Tree of the Knowledge of Good and Evil reminds Adam that in all of what he does he is responding in faith and in faithfulness to the word of God.
9. The specific command not to eat of this tree is a test of his faith. God does not ask Adam to DO something in order to earn, merit, or achieve eternal life, but NOT to do something. Obedience to this command is a pure act of faith. The issue is whether Adam will live by every word that proceeds from the mouth of God.
10. Adam believed the lie of Satan rather than the truth of God and acted accordingly. Unbelief led to the disobedience that plunged the whole human race into sin, condemnation and death. (Israel follows the same pattern of unbelief and disobedience [Deuteronomy 9:23; Hebrews 3:18, 19].)
11. The plan of redemption is designed to recreate, renew, and restore the covenant union between God and his people with its two parts, promise and obligation, that God intended from the beginning.
12. God carries out his plan through a series of historical covenants that prepare for and unfold the way of salvation through Jesus Christ revealed in the new covenant.
13. The historical covenants culminate in the fulfilment of the promise in Revelation 21:3, 'Now the dwelling of God is with men, and he will live with them. They will be his people, and God himself will be with them and be their God.

There are laudable concerns in Shepherd's approach. He wants to avoid legalism and antinomianism, but seemingly he does what

Richard Baxter (1615–91) did and turns the gospel into a new law. Shepherd wants to indicate a path which corrects distortions he considers exist in both Protestant and Roman Catholic positions, but seemingly leads us back to a medieval theology of faith and works. He wants to stress God's covenant and faithfulness in it, obedience which is never meritorious, but seemingly Jesus is easily viewed as the model man of faith and the imputation of his righteousness to the believer is not affirmed. Shepherd's thought, like Stam's, is underpinned by the idea that any concept of works or merit in the covenant relationship, whether with Adam, Christ or believers, is alien to Scripture and essentially self-righteous/legalistic in nature. In this respect his position is like the Barthian/Torrance school. It is perhaps significant that Shepherd did some studies under Berkouwer.[29]

Shepherd shows minimal interaction with classic positions.[30] The covenant is defined in terms of mutual love and faithfulness. Certainly Shepherd affirms Adam has an obligation in the covenant, but then neither the life he has received nor the life he is promised

---

29 Shepherd writes (to R.S.Ward 4 March 2003): 'We need to repudiate the idea that salvation is ultimately based on the merit of good works. Salvation is not and cannot be based on anything we can do for ourselves even theoretically. The gospel is beautifully summarised for us in Lord's Day 1 of the Heidelberg Catechism. I belong to my faithful Saviour Jesus Christ who "has fully paid for all my sins with his precious blood, and has set me free from the tyranny of the devil." These are the three points that we find in the words of our Lord in Jeremiah 31 and Hebrews 8, "I will be their God, and they will be my people." "I will forgive their wickedness and will remember their sins no more." "I will put my laws in their minds and write them on their hearts." These are the blessings that are ours through Jesus Christ in the new covenant.' This is the heart of what Shepherd wants to say about salvation. It's in other matters that problems are evident.

30 Norman Shepherd, *The Call of Grace*, 25–26, cites Charles Hodge in support of the works/merit principle, and 'the idea that perfect obedience merits the reward of eternal life as a matter of simple justice.' That Hodge alone is cited is interesting (see page 194 above)—Hoeksema does the same—and evidences a lack of interest in setting out the mainstream classic position.

are clearly connected to an obedient probation. The obligation in the covenant for the believer today is the same obligation Adam had pre-fall. In short, Christ has secured forgiveness by his death but logically we are put in a position where our covenant faithfulness is the way to salvation. It is certainly logical that a straightforward doctrine of forensic justification does not appear.

Is his position out of the limits envisaged by the WCF? The WCF clearly teaches Christ is regarded as a covenant head, whose obedience is imputed to us representatively but Shepherd does not affirm the imputation of Christ's obedience in his life to the believer, while his faith/faithfulness language makes it easy to think in terms of a dual instrumentality of faith and works in justification. (1) Those few in the 17th century who scrupled the imputation of Christ's obedience in his life did so on the grounds that to accept it might give excuse for the casual attitude to sanctification then current in society, but it has implications. (2) Shepherd's emphasis on saving faith being an obedient faith has the merit of recognising saving faith is 'not alone in the person justified' (WCF 11.2) but looks ambiguous or ambivalent when 'faithfulness' language replaces 'faith' in the preceding words of the WCF: 'Faith...is the alone instrument of instrument of justification'. (3) The rejection of the covenant of works/life as involving obedience has already been noted. Other matters could be noted but these suffice for present purposes.[31]

---

31 Worthwhile is Jeong Koo Jeon, *Covenant Theology: John Murray's and Meredith Kline's Response to the Historical Development of Federal Theology in Reformed Thought* (Lanham, MD: University Press of America, 1999), and the review by Tim J. R. Trumper in *Westminster Theological Journal* 63 (2002), 387–404. Ian Hewitson, *Trust and Obey: Norman Shepherd and the Justification Controversy at Westminster Theological Seminary*. Minneapolis MN, NextStep Resources, 2011) presents a defence of Shepherd.

Justification

As regards the covenant of works and justification by faith, the concern must be that any weakening of emphasis or confusion on obedience as the way to the highest blessing for Adam has to have repercussions.

1. It affects our understanding of Christ's obedience for us, for if perfect obedience to God was not required of Adam why should it be required of Jesus? This is the key issue, not the presence of God's kindness, love and support (which should be recognised in regard to both Adams), nor debate over the precise meaning of 'merit'.

2. If the covenant with Adam did not involve a probation arrangement in which obedience would gain eternal life in glory, there is no beyond-probation state for Adam, but only continuation in the same state as continued obedience is given. On this view one might expect Christ's saving work to return us to an Adam-like position of perpetual insecurity, whereas in fact, we have eternal life in Christ. How is this lack of correspondence to be explained? If the obedience required of Adam did not have in view the attainment of the eschatological life secured by the obedience of Jesus, then what Jesus as the Last Adam did was at least in part not necessitated by our sin. To my mind there needs to be some stress on the promise of eternal life in glory in the Adamic covenant or else the instability noted will be resolved by weakening the mediatorial work of Christ.

3. Justification is not simply the believer being treated as if he had not sinned, but as if he had fully obeyed; it includes forgiveness of sins and a right to eternal life, and adoption into God's family.

Thus the obedience of Christ in his life, as well as his obedience in his suffering the penalty of the broken covenant, comes into its own. William Cunningham (1805–61), the great Scottish theologian, says somewhere that 'the righteousness of God is the righteousness which the righteousness of God requires him to require'. This perfect righteousness is found outside of us, in Jesus Christ the Righteous One.

4. The obedience both Adam and Jesus owed was obedience springing from faith and trust in God according to covenant. Adam disobeyed, Jesus fully obeyed. The sinner is called to faith in Christ, to union and communion with him in all the virtue of his saving acts. Our confidence is always in Jesus Christ, the Lord our Righteousness, the Last Adam.

5. True faith works through love. Good works are fruits of the new relationship not means of establishing it. 'Paul fights against dead works and James wages a campaign against a dead faith', writes Bavinck.[32] A kind of ultra-Protestantism (really antinomianism) can speak of being justified by faith alone and be careless about good works. Rome speaks of being justified on the ground of faith and works. A biblical emphasis will make the careful distinction Calvin gives: 'Faith without works does not justify, but faith justifies without works.'[33]

B.B. Warfield put it well in 1911: 'Justification by Faith, we see, is not to be set in contradiction to justification by Works. It is set in contradiction only to justification by our Own Works. It

32 H. Bavinck, *Reformed Dogmatics*, Vol. 4, 223.

33 J. Calvin, *Commentaries on the Prophet Ezekiel, Vol. II* (Grand Rapids: Baker Book House, 1979), 238 (on Ezekiel 18:14–17). Note also the fine statement in the *Irish Articles* (1615) on page 65, and in the Reformation Confessions and Catechisms.

is justification by Christ's Works. The whole question, accordingly, is whether we can hope to be received into God's favour on the ground of what we do ourselves, or only on the ground of what Christ does for us. If we expect to be received on the ground of what we do ourselves—that is what is called Justification by Works. If on the ground of what Christ has done for us—that is what is meant by Justification by Faith. Justification by Faith means, that it to say, that we look to Christ and to him alone for salvation, and come to God pleading Christ's death and righteousness as the ground of our hope to be received into his favour. If Justification by Faith is out of date, that means, then, that salvation by Christ is out of date. There is nothing, in that case, left to us but that each man must just do the best he can to save himself.'[34]

Minimising the difference between the pre-fall and post fall covenant seems to mean you get more 'grace' before the fall and less grace afterward. Our covenantal obedience is emphasised as the way of maintaining the covenant relationship and inheriting its blessings.[35]

Of course, Shepherd is not to blame for conclusions others have drawn which he rejects, but overall his formulation does not commend itself as one that does justice to the biblical material or the contours of the Reformed position. Neither the Seminary nor Shepherd's Presbytery adjudged him in error, although significant polarisation occurred from 1975 when his views became of public note and he was removed from his teaching post in 1981. He transferred from the Orthodox Presbyterian Church to the

34 B.B.Warfield, *Selected Shorter Writings, Vol 1* (Nutley, NJ: Presbyterian & Reformed, 1970), 283–284.

35 The last two sentences use language suggested by comments of Prof. Cornelis P. Venema of *Mid-America Reformed Seminary*, to R.S.Ward, 3 March 2003.

Christian Reformed Church of North America, and retired in 2001. He had association with the movement that became known as the **Federal Vision** in 2002. It too was a reactive movement to prevailing superficiality and subjectivism in evangelicalism in a number of areas, including church and sacraments, with leaders like Douglas Wilson (who in 2017 declared he no longer identified with it), James B. Jordan and P. Andrew Sandlin, but was not unified on all matters. A number of denominational Synods/Assemblies passed rulings against its teaching on justification, including the Orthodox Presbyterian Church, the Presbyterian Church in America and the United Reformed Churches.[36]

The New Perspective on Paul

This movement, dating from the 1970s, is associated with names such as E.P. Sanders, James D.G. Dunn and **N.T. Wright**. Tom Wright (b. 1948), formerly the Anglican Bishop of Durham, has a conservative evangelical background, and is a prodigious writer of both popular and scholarly books. The new perspective presents a fresh appraisal of first century Judaism, arguing that it was not a religion of works-righteousness. Accordingly, the pre-Christian Paul was not a man looking to gain merit with God any more than other Jews. Rather, Jews believed that by God's gracious covenant with Abraham they were born into God's family. You did not enter the covenant relationship because of merit, but faithful obedience was required in response to God's grace in order to remain in the covenant.

36 A good overview of the issues is Guy P. Waters, *The Federal Vision and Covenant Theology: A Comparative Analysis* (Phillipsburg, Pa.: P & R,, 2006)

It follows that Paul's teaching on justification should not be seen in the way Luther and the Reformers saw it, that is, related to how a person is right before God. Paul was not opposing self-righteousness or merit theology, so much as the Jews' exclusive attitude and outlook. They thought God's covenant was only for them. This meant they used the Jewish 'works of the law'—regarded as circumcision, the purity and food laws—as 'identity markers' to exclude others from God's family. The conflict between Paul and the Jews was over how Jews and Gentiles should relate to each other within the new covenant community, not over how an individual is justified before God.

For Wright, justification is not the declaration that believers are righteous through Christ's saving work imputed to them and received through faith alone. Rather, it is the declaration that those who belong to God's family belong to it on the basis of their faith in, and obedience to, the risen Lord, and not on the basis of Jewish or other distinctives. They will be vindicated on the last day. Wright would contend that historic Protestantism and the Roman Catholic Church have both fundamentally misunderstood the true significance of justification and should rethink their positions. Thus, Wright's New Perspective on Paul [NPP].

However, this picture, presented by NPP, of first century Judaism and of crucial New Testament texts is highly questionable. Of course, true Old Testament Judaism was not a religion of merit but of grace, yet it is clear that distortions of the nature of the faith of Israel did exist. It was this reality of those seeking to establish their own righteousness rather than submitting to the righteousness of God (Rom. 10:3) that was the Jews' undoing. The majority of the Jews rejected Jesus as the messenger of the covenant (Mal. 3:1), and its very substance (Isa. 42:6). By doing so, they repudiated the covenant with Abraham, and, consequently, they had no Seed of the Woman, no Last Adam, who would recapitulate Israel and fulfil all righteousness. It is the history of Israel in the Old Testament, of the many Jews in the New Testament period, and of the Christian church, that demonstrates how easily grace can be on one's lips when self–righteousness is in one's heart.

It is exceedingly difficult to suppose that Paul's indictment of all humanity, both Jew and Gentile, in Romans 1–3 provides us with any opportunity to limit 'the works of the law' to Jewish distinctives. The application must be extended to all that God requires of us, whether we are Jews or Gentiles. Further, the Mosaic law required much more than circumcision and food and purity laws. It was a total package. The 'Judaisers' attitude to circumcision was symptomatic of a certain approach, and belief, of what constitutes a right standing before God that is antithetical to the New Testament insistence that we are justified through faith and not by works.

The subtle but highly significant shift by the NPP position, as Wright presents it, can be assessed as very like the neonomianism of the early 18th century, in which the gospel was made a new law: God justifies when he sees faith in us. 'For all its laboured originality, this theory completely fails to escape the gravitational pull of the religion of self–justification. Wright's basic thrust is that justification is no legal fiction: the believer is righteous. This righteousness may be the result of grace and of the Spirit's work within us, but when all is said and done it is our own personal righteousness. It is inherent, not imputed. We are asked to stand on the rock of our own covenant-keeping. Could that have given

Martin Luther peace? Could it give any of us peace? On the contrary our hope would ebb and flow with rise and fall in the tide of our spiritual personality.'[37]

All that was threatened against the First Adam fell on Jesus. He wore the crown of thorns that speaks of the curse (Gen. 3:18). Having borne our sin, 'he was raised for our justification'. The resurrection showed Jesus to be righteous and accepted by the Father. He was justified having fulfilled all God's law required. In his death believers died, in his resurrection they too are justified—raised with him and seated with him in heavenly places. Forgiveness for the breach of God's law together with eternal life as held out in the Adamic covenant, is God's free gift through faith in his Son, together with adoption into God's family. These vital and precious evangelical truths are appropriately secured in our thinking as we appreciate Jesus is the Last Adam, his obedience in his life and in his death dealing effectively with the consequence of the First Adam's disobedience. 'For just as through the disobedience of the one man the many were made sinners, so also through the obedience of the one man the many will be made righteous' (Rom. 5:19).

New Covenant Theology

New Covenant theology [NCT] emerged in the work of Jon Zens (b.1945) and a few others in the late 1970s. It is associated largely with Baptists who hold Reformed convictions concerning God's sovereign grace in salvation who aim to find a middle way between Dispensationalism and Reformed Baptist Covenant Theology.

---

37 Donald Macleod, *A Faith to Live By*, 167.

Currently Fred G. Zaspel would be one of the best-known leaders of this as yet not well defined movement. There is concern to use only Bible terminology, and so 'covenant of redemption' is avoided in favour of God's 'decree' (Psalm 2:7) or 'eternal purpose' (Eph. 3:11). The term 'covenant of works' is likewise regarded as problematic and Adam's 'representative headship' is preferred. Proponents of NCT argue that, according to biblical usage, a covenant is an event in history, and the historic covenants are progressive revelations of the heavenly purpose to seal the New Covenant. The idea of one covenant of grace/several administrations is therefore faulted as putting the covenant of grace above history with specific manifestations in history, and as giving insufficient weight to the newness of the new covenant ratified by Christ.

Particular concern is expressed about regarding the Mosaic covenant as an administration of the covenant of grace, for it is considered that this does not sufficiently recognise that that covenant is fulfilled in its entirety in Christ. It is thought the door is left open to continue the Mosaic law in part in church or society, and to encourage state-church notions. Jon Zens writes, 'If we stick with the biblical presentation of one "purpose" in Christ, and a plurality of covenants in history, we will avoid the confusion of Dispensationalism's earthly-purpose-for-Israel, heavenly-purpose-for-church theory, and the unnecessary assumptions of Covenant Theology which are used to bring infants into the New Covenant church.'[38]

One ought to take such concerns seriously. However, (1) the covenantal nature of the creation, and the parallel between

38 Jon Zens' seminal essay, *'Is There a 'Covenant of Grace'?'* can be found online at his website: http://www.searchingtogether.org/articles/zens/covenant.htm

Adam and Christ as 'representative heads' who are committed to covenant work is, I think, clear from exegesis, as is the Trinitarian commitment for human redemption. If this reality is present under other terms, we should not scruple them. (2) The distinctiveness of the unfolding stages in God's historical disclosure does need to be recognised, as does legitimate criticism, but it is not obvious that mainstream Reformed Covenant Theology is guilty as charged. (3) It is probably true to say that the three-fold distinction made in the Mosaic law by Reformed theologians (cf. WCF 19.3 also Baptist Confession, 1689) which distinguished moral, civil and ceremonial laws, has been misapplied so as to somewhat blunt the New Testament teaching that the law of Moses has been superseded.[39]

On the other hand, it is a distinction that goes back a long way to the early decades of the Christian era and is capable of robust biblical defence.[40] The unique position of the moral law is seen in the fact that:

1. Only the Ten Commandments were spoken by God's voice;
2. they alone were accompanied by the shaking of Mount Sinai;
3. they alone were written by his finger;
4. they alone were written on enduring stone tablets rather than merely being written in a book (Deut. 4:10–14; Exod. 24:4) and
5. they alone of the various laws were placed in the ark of the covenant (Deut. 10:5).

39 For a useful interaction of different viewpoints see Wayne Strickland (ed.), *The Law, the Gospel and the Modern Christian* (Grand Rapids: Zondervan, 1993).

40 See the historical case outlined in Jonathan F. Bayes, *The Threefold Division of the Law* (Newcastle upon Tyne: The Christian Institute, 2017) available as a pdf at http://www.christian.org.uk/wp-content/downloads/the-threefold-division-of-the-law.pdf

6. They formed the introduction to the Mosaic covenant which, in fact, expounds them in a manner appropriate for the people at that time (Deut. 6–26).
7. Of course, they were also fully complete, the tablets being written on the front and the back, so that there was no room for other commandments of the same unique kind for there were none (Exod. 32:15), and
8. they were regarded as superior to the ceremonial law (e.g. Psalm 51:16–19; Jer. 7; Amos 5).
9. It should also be remembered that the greatest commandment, on which depends everything else, is total love for the Lord (Matt. 22:37 quoting the exposition of the first commandment in Deut. 6) and also love for one's neighbour—a command which, while explicit in a context of laws of different character, is a necessary corollary to the other given that humans bear the divine likeness (Lev. 19:18 cf. Matt. 7:12). Hence,
10. these considerations lead to the common view that the Decalogue is a reflection, in a form suited to the historical situation of Israel, of the moral law, the law of love, written on Adam's heart at his creation.

Although the ten commandments can be distinguished, Christians do not obey them because they are commanded by Moses but, rather, they receive them from Christ in the gospel who embodied them in his own life and ministry. New Covenant Theology ends up recognising that most of the ten commandments are warranted from the New Testament but, by and large, they end up dropping the sabbath commandment. Classic Covenant Theology, on the other hand, has greater clarity on the relationship of the ten commandments to the law of love, the moral law written on the heart and, also, sees the creation sabbath as having its parallel in the new creation's Lord's Day.[41]

41 For a fuller treatment see Rowland S. Ward, 'The Lord's Day and the Westminster Confession' in Anthony T. Selvaggio (ed.), *The Faith Once Delivered: Essays in Honour of Dr Wayne R. Spear* (Phillipsburg, NJ: P & R Publishing, 2007). 191–216.

BIBLIOGRAPHY

This is a listing of the principal sources used and referred to in the text.

Literature to 1800

William Ames, *Medulla Theologica* (1623) translated by J.D.Eusden as *The Marrow of Theology* (Durham NC: Labyrinth, 1983)

Augustine, *City of God, Book XVI*, Ch. 27 [NPNF] Vol.2, 326–327; *Of Marriage and Concupiscence*, Book II, Ch.24 [NPNF] Vol. 5, 292. ed P. Schaff (Peabody: Hendriksen, 1995)

John Ball, *A Short Treatise contayning all the Principall Grounds of Christian Religion, by way of questions and answers...* [Cambridge, 1615] (4th printing: London: Thomas Pauier, 1634)

John Ball, *A Treatise of the Covenant of Grace*, (London: E. Brewster, 1645)

John Barret, *Good will towards men, or A Treatise of the Covenants viz: Of works, and of grace: old and new...* (London, 1675)

Thomas Blake, *Vindiciae Foederis*, 2nd ed. (London, 1658)

Samuel Bolton, *The True Bounds of Christian Freedom* [1645] (London: Banner of Truth, 1964)

W. à Brakel, *The Christian's Reasonable Service* (Dutch 1700; ET: Pittsburg: Soli Deo Gloria, 1994f)

William Bridge, *Christ and the Covenant...* (London, 1667)

Anthony Burgess, *Vindiciae Legis, or A Vindication of the Morall Law and the Covenants...* (London: Thomas Underhill, 2nd ed. 1647)

William Bucanus, *Institutiones Theologicae* [Bremen 1605] translated by Robert Hill as *Institutions of Christian Religion* (London, 1606)

Peter Bulkeley, *The Gospel-Covenant...* (London, 1651)

Edmund Calamy, *Two solemne Covenants made betweene God and Man: viz. The Covenants of Workes, And the Covenant of Grace* (London: T. Banks, 1646)

John Calvin, *Commentaries on the Old and New Testaments*, 45 vols. (Grand Rapids: Eerdmans 1948/50)

J. Cloppenburg, *Disputationes de foedere Dei et testamento veteri et novo* (Basel, 1643).

J. Cocceius, *Summa Doctrinae de Foedere et Testamento* (Leiden, 1648)

David Dickson, *Therapeutica sacra* [Latin 1656] (Edinburgh, 1664)

J.Dod and R Cleaver, *A Plaine and familiar Exposition of the Ten Commandments, with a methodical Short Catechism...* (London: Thomas Man, 1604)

Thomas Cartwright, *A Treatise of Christian Religion* (London: T. Man, 1616)

John Downame, *The summe of sacred divinitie* (London, c. 1628)

The Works of Jonathan Edwards (Edinburgh: Bannner of Truth Trust, 1974)

Jonathan Edwards, *Treatise on Grace,* (Cambridge: James Clarke & Co., 1971)

Dudley Fenner, *Sacra Theologia* (London 1585)

Henry Finch, *The Sacred Doctrine of Divinitie Gathered Out of the Worde of God* [Middelburg: Richard Schilders, 1589] (London: Felix Kyngston, 1613)

Edward Fisher, *The Marrow of Modern Divinitie* [1](London 1645) [2](London, 1646)

John Gill, *A Body of Divinity* (1769, repr: Grand Rapids: Sovereign Grace 1971)

Patrick Gillespie, *The Ark of the Testament Opened* (London,1661)

Edward Leigh, *A Treatise of the Divine Promises* (London, 1633)

Wolfgang Musculus, *Loci Communes Sacrae Theologiae* (?Bern, 1555) trans. by John Man of Oxford as *Common Places of Christian Religion* (London, 1563)

John Owen, *An Exposition of the Epistle to the Hebrews* [ed. W.H.Goold, 1855] (Grand Rapids: Baker, 1990)

John Owen, *Biblical Theology* (Morgan, PA: Soli Deo Gloria, 1994)

William Pemble, *Vindici Fidei* (Oxford, 1629)

William Perkins, *The Golden Chaine,* [1591] in *Works* (London, 1605)

W. Perkins, *A Commentarie upon the Epistle of the Galatians* (London, 2nd ed., 1592)

W. Perkins, *An Exposition of the Creede* [1595] in *Collected Works* (London 1605)

W. Perkins, *A Reformed Catholike* [1597] in *Collected Works* (London, 1605)

A Polanus, *The Substance of Christian Religion Soundly Set Forth in two books by definitions and partitions framed according to the rules of a natural method* [translated from the Latin by Elijah Wilcocks] (London: John Oxenbridge, 1595)

John Preston, *The New Covenant* (London, 1629)

Francis Roberts, *Mysterium & Medulla Bibliorum...* (London, 1657)

Robert Rollock, *A Treatise of God's Effectual Calling,* trans. Henry Holland (London: T. Man, 1603)

Samuel Rutherford, *Covenant of Life Opened* (Edinburgh, 1655)

John Salkeld, *A Treatise of Paradise* (London: N Butter, 1617)

Obadiah Sedgwick, *The Bowels of Tender Mercy...* (London, 1661)

William Strong, *A Discourse of the Two Covenants...* (London, 1678)

John Tombes, *Two treatises and an appendix to them concerning Infant-Baptisme. The former being a Exercitation presented to the Chairman of a Committee of the Assembly of Divines...* (London, December 15, 1646)

Francis Turretin, *Institutes of Elenctic Theology* (Phillipsburg: P & R, 1992)

Zachary Ursinus, *A Collection of Certain Learned Discourses translated from the Latin text of David Pareus* by I.H. (London: J. Broome, 1600)

The Whole Works of James Ussher (Dublin, 1847–64) Vol. 1.249 [life by C.R. Elrington]

James Ussher, *The Principles of Christian religion ...*(London: Geo Badger, 1645)

James Ussher, *A Body of divinitie* (London, 1645) [a compilation not strictly by Ussher]

George Walker, *The Manifolde Wisdom of God* (London, 1641)

D. Whitby, *A paraphrase and commentary on the New Testament* (London, 1703)

Herman Witsius, *Oeconomia Foederum Dei cum homnibus* (1677) 3rd ed 1694 translated by William Cruikshank as *The Economy of the Covenants between God and Man* [1763] (London, 1822)

Johannes Wollebius, *Compendium Theologiae Christianae* translated by J.W. Beardslee, *Reformed Dogmatics* (Grand Rapids: Baker, 1965)

Literature since 1800

Dictionary of Scottish Church History and Theology (Edinburgh: T. & T. Clark, 1993)

The Infallible Word: A Symposium by members of the Faculty of Westminster Theological Seminary (Philadelphia: Presbyterian & Reformed Publ., 1967)

B.G.Armstrong, *Calvin and the Amyraut Heresy* (Wisconsin: Wisconsin University Press, 1969)

Richard C. Barcellos, *The Covenant of Works: Its Confessional and Scriptural Basis* (Palmdale, CA: Reformed Baptist Academic Press, 2016)

William Barker, *Puritan Profiles* (Fearn: Christian Focus, 1991)

Karl Barth, *Church Dogmatics III/1 & IV/1* (Edinburgh: T. & T Clark, 1956/58)

H. Bavinck, *Reformed Dogmatics* (Grand Rapids: Baker, 4 vols. 2003–2008))

J.R. Beeke, *Assurance of Faith* (New York: Peter Lang, 1994)

L. Berkhof, *Systematic Theology* (London: Banner of Truth, 1958)

G.C. Berkouwer, *Man, the Image of God* (Grand Rapids: Eerdmans, 1962)

G.C. Berkouwer, *Sin* (Grand Rapids: Eerdmans, 1971)

L.D. Bierma, *German Calvinism in the Confessional Age* (Grand Rapids: Baker, 1996)

Craig A. Blaising & Darrell L. Bock, *Progressive Dispensationalism* (Grand Rapids: Baker, 2000)

H. Blocher, *In the Beginning* (Downers Grove: IVP, 1984)

Carl W. Bogue, *Jonathan Edwards and the Covenant of Grace* (Cherry Hill, NJ: Mack Publishing, 1975)

U. Cassuto, *A Commentary on the Book of Genesis* (Jerusalem: Magnes, 1961)

Arthur C. Cochrane, *Reformed Confessions of the 16th Century* (Westminster Press, 1966)

John Coffey, *Politics, Religion and the British Revolutions: The Mind of Samuel Rutherford* (Cambridge: Cambridge University Press, 1997)

William Cunningham, *The Reformers and the Theology of the Reformation* (London: Banner of Truth, 1967)

R.L. Dabney, *Systematic Theology* (St Louis: Presbyterian Publishing, 1878)

N.Diemer, *Het Scheppingsverbond met Adam...* (Kampen: Kok, 1935)

Peter Y. de Jong, *The Covenant Idea in New England Theology 1620–1847* (Grand Rapids: Eerdmans, 1945)

G.W. Dollar, *A History of Fundamentalism in America* (Greenville: Bob Jones University Press, 1973)

D.A. Dorsey, *The Literary Structure of the Old Testament* (Baker, 1999)

W.J. Dumbrell, *Covenant and Creation* (Carlisle, UK: Paternoster, 1984)

S.G. de Graaf, *Promise and Deliverance, Vol 1* (St Catherines, Ont.:Paedia, 1977)

Howard Griffith and John R. Muether *Creator, Redeemer, Consummator: A Festschrift for Meredith G. Kline* (Greenville, SC: Reformed Academic Press/Reformed Theological Seminary, 2000)

Wayne Grudem, *Systematic Theology* (Leicester, UK: IVP, 1994)

Allan M. Harman, *Deuteronomy: The Commands of a Covenant God* (Fearn: Christian Focus, 2001)

G.D. Henderson (ed), *The Scots Confession 1560* (St Andrew Press, 1960)

H. Heppe, *Reformed Dogmatics Set Out and Illustrated from the Sources* [German 1861; English trans. by G.T. Thomson] (London: George Allen & Unwin, 1950)

A.A. Hodge, *Outlines of Theology* (1879 ed., London: Banner of Truth Trust, 1972)

A.A. Hodge, *The Confession of Faith* [1869] (London: Banner of Truth, 1968)

Charles Hodge, *Systematic Theology* (London: Thomas Nelson, 1873)

A.A. Hoekema, *Created in God's Image* (Grand Rapids: Eerdmans, 1986)

H. Hoeksema, *The Triple Knowledge, Vol 1* (Grand Rapids: Reformed Free Publishing, 1972)

Jeong Koo Jeon, *Covenant Theology: John Murray's and Meredith Kline's Response to the Historical Development of Federal Theology in Reformed Thought* (Lanham, MD: University Press of America, 1999)

Mark W. Karlberg, *Covenant Theology in Reformed Perspective* (Eugene: Wipf & Stock Publishers, 2000)

G.H.Kersten, *Reformed Dogmatics, Vol. 1* (Grand Rapids: Netherlands Ref, 1980)

Ernest Kevan, *The Grace of Law* (London: Carey Kingsgate Press, 1964)

M.G. Kline, *By Oath Consigned* (Grand Rapids: Eerdmans, 1968)

M.G. Kline, *Images of the Spirit* (Grand Rapids: Baker, 1980)

Abraham Kuyper, *E Voto Dordraceno, Vol. 2* (Amsterdam, 1895)

D.C. Lachman, *The Marrow Controversy* (Edinburgh: Rutherford House, 1988)

J. Laidlaw, *The Bible Doctrine of Man* (Edinburgh: T & T Clark, 1879)

Peter A. Lillback, *The Binding of God* (Grand Rapids: Baker, 2001)

John L. Mackay, *Exodus* (Fearn: Mentor, 2001)

Donald Macleod, *A Faith to Live By* (Fearn: Christian Focus, 2002)

Hugh Martin, *The Atonement in its relations to the Covenant, the Priesthood, the Intercession of our Lord* (Edinburgh: Knox Press, 1976)

David McKay, *The Bond of Love* (Fearn: Christian Focus, 2001).

Richard A.Muller, *God, Creation and Providence in the Thought of Jacob Arminius* (Grand Rapids: Baker, 1991)

Richard A. Muller, *Post-Reformation Reformed Dogmatics* (Grand Rapids: Baker, 2003)

Collected Writings of John Murray, Vol. 2 (Edinburgh: Banner of Truth, 1977)

Daniel Neal, *The History of the Puritans* (London: William Baynes & Son, 1822)

D.N.J. Poole, *Stages of Religious Faith in the Classical Reformation Tradition* (Lewiston: Mellon, 1995)

Samuel D. Renihan, *From Shadow to Substance: The Federal Theology of the English Particular Baptists 1642–1704* (Oxford: Centre for Baptist History and Heritage, 2018)

Robert L. Reymond, *A New Systematic Theology of the Christian Faith* (Nashville: Nelson, 1998)

O. Palmer Robertson, *The Christ of the Covenants* (Phillipsburg, NJ: P & R, 1980)

Holmes Rolston III, *John Calvin versus the Westminster Confession* (Richmond, VA: John Knox Press, 1972)

P. & D.S. Schaff (eds.), *Creeds of Christendom* (New York: Harper & Row, 1931)

K. Schilder, *Het Verbond in de Gereformeerde Symbolen* [Syllabus, 1941–42]

W.G.T. Shedd, *Dogmatic Theology, Vol 2* (New York: Scribners, 1889)

N. Shepherd, *The Call of Grace* (Phillipsburg, NJ: P & R Publishing, 2000)

J.H. Skilton (ed.), *The Law and the Prophets* (Nutley: Presbyterian & Ref., 1974)

Morton H. Smith, *Systematic Theology, Vol. 1* (Greenville, SC: Greenville Seminary Press, 1994)

G.J. Spykman, *Reformational Theology* (Grand Rapids: Eerdmans, 1992)

C. Stam, *The Covenant of Love* (Winnipeg: Premier Publishing, 1999)

S. Strehle, *Calvinism, Federalism and Scholasticism* (Bern: Peter Lang, 1988)

Wayne Strickland (ed.), *The Law, the Gospel and the Modern Christian* (Grand Rapids: Zondervan, 1993)

Collected Writings of James Henley Thornwell, Vol 1 (Banner of Truth, 1974)

Selected Journal Articles

Crawford Gribben, 'The Eschatology of the Puritan Confessions' in *Scottish Bulletin of Evangelical Theology* 20:1 (Spring 2002) 51–78.

Donald Macleod, 'Federal Theology: An Oppressive Legalism?' in *The Banner of Truth*, 125 (February 1974) 21–28.

M. McGiffert, 'From Moses to Adam: The Making of the Covenant of Works' in *The Sixteenth Century Journal*, XIX. 2 (Summer 1988) 131–155.

D.M. McIntyre, 'First Strictures on the Marrow of Modern Divinity' in *The Evangelical Quarterly*, X (1938) 61–70.

S.Mechie, 'Education for the Ministry in Scotland Since the Reformation' in *Records of the Scottish Church History Society* XV.1 (1963) 1–20.

Richard A. Muller, 'Covenant and Conscience in English Reformed Theology' in *Westminster Theological Journal* XLII.2 (Spring 1980) 308–344.

Richard A. Muller, 'The Federal Motif in Seventeenth Century Arminian Theology' in *Nederlands Archief voor Kerkgescheidenis* 62, 1 (1982) 102–122.

Gary L. Nebeker, 'John Nelson Darby and Trinity College, Dublin: A Study in Eschatological Contrasts' in *Fides et Historia*, XXIV.2 (Summer/Fall 2002) 87f.

Geoffrey Thomas, 'Alexander Comrie' in *Banner of Truth Magazine* 65 (Feb 1969) 4–8; #66 (Mar 1969) 29–35.

James B. Torrance, 'The Contribution of McLeod Campbell to Scottish Theology' in *Scottish Journal of Theology* 26 (1973) 295–311.

Cornelis P. Venema, 'Recent Criticisms of the Covenant of Works in the Westminster Confession of Faith' in *Mid-America Journal of Theology*, 9:1 (Fall 1993) 165–198.

SCRIPTURE INDEX

INDEX OF NAMES AND SUBJECTS